LETTERS FROM THE LEELANAU

LETTERS FROM THE LEELANAU

Essays of People and Place

KATHLEEN STOCKING

Ann Arbor

THE UNIVERSITY OF MICHIGAN PRESS

1994   1993   1992   1991   8   7   6   5

Library of Congress Cataloging-in-Publication Data

Stocking, Kathleen, 1945–
    Letters from the Leelanau : essays of people and place / Kathleen
Stocking.
        p.   cm.
    ISBN 0-472-09445-9. — ISBN 0-472-06445-2 (pbk.)
    1. Leelanau County (Mich.)—Social life and customs.   2. Leelanau
County (Mich.)—Description and travel.   I. Title.
F572.L45S75   1990
977.4'635—dc20   90-35596
                                                                        CIP

Many of these pieces appeared, in various forms and at various times,
in the following magazines, and I would like to thank the editors of
each: *Detroit Monthly; Metropolitan Detroit; West Michigan Magazine;
Traverse, the Magazine; Michigan, the Magazine of the Detroit News; Detroit, the Magazine of the Detroit Free Press; the Cincinnati Enquirer;
D.A.C., the Magazine of the Detroit Athletic Club;* and *Travel and Leisure.*

Special acknowledgment is made to the Michigan Council for the Arts
for its support of this book and its 1989 Creative Artist award to the
author.

Illustrations by Mary Harney

Map drawn by Grace Dickinson, Glen Arbor, Michigan.
© 1989 Grace Dickinson.

Cover illustration: *Manitou Dreams*
by David P. Grath (47″ x 47″ oil on canvas).
From the private collection of Beverly
Gilmore.

*This book is dedicated to
the people of Leelanau County*

When from the long distant past nothing subsists, after the people are dead, after the things are broken and scattered, still alone, more fragile, but with more vitality, more unsubstantial, yet more persistent, more faithful, the smell and taste of things, remain poised for a long time, like souls, ready to remind us, waiting and hoping for their moment, amid the ruins of all the rest and bear unfalteringly, in the almost impalpable drop of their essence, the vast structure of recollection.

—Marcel Proust

Preface and Acknowledgments

A few years ago I came home from New York City to a farmhouse at the base of the Sleeping Bear Dunes. The farmhouse had once belonged to a woman, then in her seventies, who lived down the road from me. Her husband had died in a farm accident while she was still a young bride, and she had moved then—had had to move—with her farmhand into the kind of house that real estate agents describe as a handyman's special. After that, she always called the farmhand her renter. And it was this former farmhand, himself a man in his seventies when I met him, who used to come by the house that had been hers to check on me. I needed checking on. I was alone with two small children and felt in danger of being buried alive by the dune behind my house, by the culture I'd escaped only to be brought back to it with a thwack, like one of those little rubber balls attached to a wooden paddle by a long rubberband.

It was in this farmhouse that I learned to love the peninsula I'd earlier left. The intense shadows on full moon nights. The sound of the grass. The early morning sun shining on the dunes behind the house reflecting back pink and gold hammered air everywhere. The wild turkeys that came up onto the porch to eat the corn my neighbor gave me to feed them. That farmhouse is no longer there; even the wood violets that used to bloom around the foundation are gone because they needed the shade the house provided in order to grow. But it was in that farmhouse that this book began.

I would like to express my thanks to people who helped with this book, many of them indirectly, by helping me to sustain and to become a writer. First there is Donald Hall at the University of Michigan, who let me join his poetry writing class when I had not yet written any poems but only thought I could. I am grateful, too, to the following people: Jim Vesely, Kirk Cheyfitz, Bob Pisor, Ruth Coughlin, and Lee Ann Schreiner, editors and writers in Detroit who offered encouragement at various points along the way; Bob Root, a professor at Central Michigan University, Gretchen Millich at National Public Radio's *All Things Considered,* and Stephen Ward at NPR in Lansing for making me feel "discovered"; and writers Beverly Gilmore and Gloria Whelan for moving north and being my friends. Thanks also to writer and neighbor Jim Harrison for his sense of humor in a dark hour, and to my editor at *Detroit Monthly,* Diane Brozek, for her warmth, wisdom, loyalty, and professionalism through the years.

I would like to express my gratitude to Mary Erwin, my editor at the University of Michigan Press, for her awareness of the Leelanau Peninsula and enthusiasm about the Leelanau essays. Thanks also to her assistant, Andrew Fisk, for his willing attention to detail and his professionalism; to the writers and professors who read the manuscript for the University of Michigan Press and who were sincere and helpful in their responses; and to artist David Grath, illustrator Mary Harney, graphic designer Laurie Davis, mapmaker and artist Grace Dickinson, and photographer Minnie Wabanimkee for their invaluable contributions to this book.

This book would not have been possible without the financial support of the Michigan Council for the Arts, which awarded me its Creative Artist award in 1989. I would also like to thank friend and poet Steve Tudor, a professor in the English Department at Wayne State University, for teaching me how to write a grant. Writers Stuart Dybek, Jim Harrison, Janet Kauffman, and David Lawrence, Jr., were supportive when they reviewed an early proposal for the book and commented favorably.

In my everyday encounters beyond the writing world I have found support for this book as well. Grace Glynn, a longtime friend and mother of thirteen, has mothered me and typed for me for years; because I am dyslexic, I was—until recently when I began working on a computer—helpless to produce decent manuscripts without her. A cyclamen I once gave her bloomed repeatedly for what seemed like an eternity because, I'm convinced, it knew it was in the house of a saint.

I owe many thanks also to Charles Lockwood, a computer programmer, a kindly genius and infinitely patient man who programmed my computer and got me started, something I could never have done on my own. Gerry Barczak, the Duane and Ellen Beard family, Ron Boyer, Bill Corbett, Marcia Couturier, Rebecca and Linus Couturier, Leah Frankel, Virgil Gradowski, Jim Hunt, Lila Hunter, T. J. Johnston, Eric Keller, Helen Knapp, Suzanne Latta, Kathy McCarthy, Margo Million, Dave Murphy, Jim Olson, Eva Petosky, Gene and Marie Petroskey, Kate Piskor, Duncan and Maggie Sprattmoran, Douglas Szot, Dwayne Szot, Terry Tarnow, Teresa Walter, Dr. George Wagoner, Ray Welch, Delores Wilcox, and Eugene Wilcox were the right people in the right place at the right time in my life; I don't know where I'd be without them. I would also like to thank my friends Char Verschave, Geradine Simkins, and Larry Doe and their children for being my extended family.

Finally, special thanks to my mother, Eleanor Stocking, for sharing with me her love of books and writing, and to my children, Jesse, Lilah, and Gaia, for all their love, all the laughing; there could have been no writing without them.

Introduction

The essays in *Letters from the Leelanau* focus on people or events on the Leelanau Peninsula in the decade between 1979 and 1989. All are written from the perspective of someone who has grown up on the Leelanau Peninsula, moved away, and come back to live here again.

Some of these essays have appeared in other forms in various Detroit periodicals and magazines throughout the 1980s. These have been edited for inclusion in *Letters from the Leelanau,* and other essays have been written specifically for the book, with the overall idea of creating a balanced portrait of the peninsula.

The pieces are not arranged chronologically, but according to kind. A friend who scanned the four subheadings in the table of contents—"Close to the Village," "When the Mists Part," "Contemplating the Shadows of Sturgeon," and "Personals"— said I had written about outer reality, inner reality, physical space, and mental space. Maybe, but there was no plan. I just wrote about where I was, because it was where I was, and the groupings occurred naturally.

Because the essays were written at different times and not organized according to time they overlap in places, and there are small repetitions and my neighbors who appear in "Village Life" appear again in "Graduation Day—Lake Leelanau St. Mary's." My friends appear and reappear, and the same person may have a walk-on part in two or three different essays. Thus the way the essays have been gathered creates a kind of fugue.

This was not intentional, but it does in some way capture the mood of life on the peninsula.

Lives overlap here. People are interrelated through successive generations. You don't dare gossip about anyone because you're probably talking to his or her cousin. Roads overlap too, and many people have remarked that they often get lost on this peninsula, even after living here for years. I sometimes get lost myself. The roads follow the lines of the lakes and hills, and this does not lead you in a straight line but sometimes seemingly in circles. To further confuse matters, sometimes the name of a road will change midway so as not to slight either of two people who might have lived on the road and for whom the road might have been named.

The Leelanau Peninsula is a sweet place, a pretty place, a place that seems to always have inspired people. It inspired Henry Schoolcraft to name it Leelanau, a word he said was Indian, and he invented a legend about a beautiful lost Indian daughter by that name. People to this day will tell you that Leelanau is an Indian word meaning "land of delight," or "beautiful lost daughter." In fact the local Ottawa Indians had no *l* in their language, and Leelanau is not an Indian word, as far as I know, and has no meaning other than that which Schoolcraft assigned it.

Others have also been inspired to invent or envision or prophesy about the peninsula. I have heard that the Leelanau Peninsula will be the site of the Second Coming of Christ, with the next Messiah to be born on a peninsula at the forty-fifth parallel—right about where the roadside picnic table is, north of Suttons Bay. Those who study electromagnetic fields say the Leelanau is "a center for energy." And the Federal Emergency Management Agency report lists this as "a host area" in case of nuclear attack; it advises those in Detroit to come north, drive slowly, and bring their dogs with them because we here will be building kennels for their pets. Perhaps all of these myths and legends and fantasies about the Leelanau Peninsula are, as much as anything, a testament to the way the delicate beauty of the place touches people's imaginations.

I grew up here, at a time when you could find Petoskey stones by the bushel on the beach, and then the peninsula truly was a pristine place, like those fabled destinations that exist "east of the sun and west of the moon." But since then it's been discovered by tourists and condominium developers, and the beautiful, soft Leelanau of my childhood is gone. No, I shouldn't say "gone." It's there in rare moments, in predawn summer privacy, in winter some 2:00 A.M. when the northern lights flare up, their rainbow flames licking the Bible-black sky; well, then, sometimes.

I came back to this peninsula in part because it was what I knew, and in 1974 I needed to be where I knew my surroundings. I'd gone to school in Ann Arbor at the University of Michigan during the height of the radical sixties, when the campus was a centrifuge or crucible of cultural change that spun out and spewed out and used up more of my friends and fellow students than I can bear to remember. After that I'd lived in Manhattan, a no-man's-land by most people's standards. As a friend said once while visiting me there, "Manhattan is a place where you feel like you're moving even when you're standing still."

So I'd moved back to the Leelanau Peninsula, into a little house on a little road. I needed land and country around me so I could feel I belonged to something bigger than myself. I needed birds and trees and the observable minutiae of seasons so I could feel my life as a stream of little movements. I needed huge hills and big lakes and that sense of panorama and distance that living on a peninsula gives one. I needed this place, this known place, because I knew it was not illusory. And, without thinking about it and primarily because people asked me to, I began to write about it.

It seems to me that as I've been writing about the peninsula, what people want to know is what life is really like here. "Write about your village, your neighbors, write about normal life," one Detroit editor used to exhort me. It dawned on me that her yardstick of what "normal life" was like in a small, rural community was vague, perhaps becoming more vague all the time from her vantage point in a chaotic urban setting, and she wanted me to provide her and the readers with a reality touchstone.

This notion of my life as a measure of the normal always amused me, since, like many writers, I consider myself (and not a few of my nonwriting neighbors) to be fairly eccentric. It is also a source of continuing amazement to me that so many people who are at least a generation or two away from the farm often imagine a rural setting for themselves, perhaps one described to them by their grandparents or experienced by them on vacations, as a reference point for real life.

It is our context that gives our lives meaning, but with the character of America changing so rapidly, sometimes it's hard to know what that context is. Columnist Ellen Goodman, who writes for the *Boston Globe,* observed a while ago, "We urban people consider ourselves transients in our communities. We don't sink our roots in." So somebody has to take on the job of staying in one place long enough to keep track of the issues, to tell what passes for normal, to provide a compass point in an America that is changing so fast that the closest thing to a shared culture seems to be the rural setting we all came from a hundred years or so ago.

On some level, we all want to pick berries, hunt and fish, milk cows, and harvest wheat with a hand sickle. The Irish fishermen's smocks that are advertised in the *New Yorker* every week are not being sold to Irish fishermen, but to people who want to be, even for a moment, Irish fishermen. I sometimes think the transition from a hunting and gathering and agricultural and seafaring culture to an urban, industrial, technological one was too fast for most of us. Our biology, or our neuropaths, haven't caught up yet. We get water from the tap, but we want to haul it from the well.

Michael Sendal, writing in the *New Republic* in February 1988, in an article entitled "Democrats and Community," observed that "The flow of power to large-scale institutions coincided with the decline of families and neighborhoods, . . . leaving the individual to confront the impersonal forces of the economy and the state without the moral or political resources that intermediate communities." Sendal, who teaches in the Department of Government at Harvard University, concludes, "What Reagan stirred was a yearning for a way of life that seems to be receding in recent times—a common life of larger meanings, on a smaller, less impersonal scale than the nation-state provides."

A lot of the people who came to the Leelanau in the last twenty years were not all Reaganites by any means but they were trying to create, or recreate, what Sendal calls "a common life of larger meanings, on a smaller, less impersonal scale." This country has always had a "little house on the prairie" sense of itself, no matter that since the turn of the century ninety percent of the people live in cities. Some of us in this country did grow up on farms, of course, but the sense that we did, as a nation, is more prevalent than the fact that we did.

Writer Gloria Whelan, who has won an O. Henry Award and numerous Pushcart Prizes and who is a "rural" Michigan writer, has a character in a recent short story who wonders how Henry David Thoreau managed to convince himself that he was alone in the wilderness at Walden Pond, even though he walked to town every day—a mile away—and people dropped in all the time. A literary conceit, perhaps, and also what readers wanted to believe, even in those relatively untrammeled times, as Thoreau no doubt astutely intuited.

People like the idea that somebody is living out of the maelstrom, even if they aren't. We crave calm; we're starved for "everydayness." All one has to do is open the pages of any magazine to find items that will add "country charm" to any home. The bucolic life, the pastoral idyll, is within reach of anyone who can afford a flour sack dish towel or a graniteware coffee pot. The need for people to be able to hear about and imagine a place in the country, a time of innocence where, for instance, kids aren't shooting kids, is in part the need that regional writing serves, the way during the Depression movies about rich people satisfied people's needs to fantasize about the things they wanted but couldn't buy.

But today, as my reclusive neighbor, writer Jim Harrison, said once about living on the Leelanau Peninsula, "There's no escaping anything anymore." Those of us who live here take planes and use computers, just like everyone else. We've had people die of AIDS here. Some people beat their children. The same dioxin that's in the disposable baby diapers in the landfills in New Jersey is in the baby diapers in the landfills here. Our landfills are full to overflowing, and some of our groundwater is polluted. Et cetera. It would be more than a literary device, it would be sheer chicanery to pretend otherwise. It would be phony for me to pretend to be more "farmy" than I am. Although I grew up on the Leelanau Peninsula and have lived here most of my life, I also spent seven years in Ann Arbor and five in Manhattan. I also regularly leave here, have friends everywhere, and listen to the news.

Still, it is daunting to know that people crave calm, crave rusticity, and not give in to that. What I do instead is try to meet the need for people to know what rural life is like, without withholding from the writing my awareness of what's going on in the rest of the world.

We are, of course, somewhat isolated on the Leelanau Peninsula—geographically and in other ways as well, which is not the same thing as living without cognizance of what's going on. Living on the Leelanau Peninsula is a little like staying back home when there's a war going on: we hear what's happening at The Front, but we aren't *there*. Instinctively we know that our loved ones in the trenches need to know if Mary Jane's had her baby, if the potato crop is in, and if the geese have gone south yet. Their knowing these things, we understand, will help them deal with the reality of *their* lives, out there in the urban mine fields alone.

My perception of the world as a churning sea of troubles, as a place at war with itself, is not unique to me. Pick up almost any periodical and you can come across something in this vein. Tom Shales, writing in an October 1987 *Esquire,* says, "The Eighties are not good times. They are bad times masquerading as good times. Any minute now, blooey. Oooh, what pain. . . . Threats multiply geometrically: the Reds, the missiles, the Bomb, terrorist attacks, freeway snipers, sexually transmitted diseases. A pit bull could eat your face. The next midair collision is just beyond the next cloud."

In the same issue of *Esquire,* Dave Remnick of the *Washington Post* writes about the newspaper *USA Today* as the "good news is no news" paper, the paper that caters to the flying class, "a hurried, self-involved" group that "like all people who travel, at times feel as if they are everywhere and nowhere, disconnected." The point is, whether we read *USA Today* or not, whether we fly all the time or not, we all feel at times as if we're "everywhere and nowhere at once, disconnected." It is the mode—and mood—of the times.

I was not the only person in the United States in the late 1970s who wanted to return to the place where I'd grown up, to find again the basic rhythms of human existence. In many ways it was the signature of a generation, of a decade, and many others were doing the same thing then, both on the Leelanau Peninsula and around the nation. I thought I would be alone in my return, an eccentric person doing an eccentric thing, but I found that I was part of the efflux from cities and suburbs. As so often happens, just when you think you have an original idea, you discover you're part of a trend.

I met and married an Ottawa Indian man in 1979 just as I was beginning work on the Leelanau essays and he is the man I refer to as my husband throughout the book. We were together nearly ten years, developing and sharing a closeness to each other and to the mysticism of the Native American culture. The intense intimacy we had known at first, however, did not continue, and as the decade of the eighties came to a close, we were no longer together.

Many of the people who had journeyed to the Leelanau to create a new life-style for themselves also found that their most intimate relationships and friendships could not sustain either the idealism or the work of exploring new directions, and they parted, returned to cities, awoke one morning to find that the golden light that had bathed everything in possibility had faded irrevocably.

The Leelanau Peninsula has often been compared to the mythical Isle of Avalon, that place off the coast of England where fairies live, summer is eternal, and King Arthur still holds court in Camelot. The kind of place where you could pull the sword Excalibur from the stone.

But places that engender great hopes and dreams are often evanescent. Leelanau became in the seventies and eighties a place of escape, as people seeking to get away from the crime and pollution and anomie of cities discovered the peninsula. It was strange for me to live in a place being discovered, to become friends with the discoverers, to share their joy in discovery, and yet to remain in everyday contact with my old friends and neighbors from my growing-up years, and go to the same pancake suppers I'd always gone to, and walk in the same dunes I always walked in; it was and is like living in a place that is both foreign and familiar, like rubbing your head and patting your belly at the same time.

This phenomenon in the eighties of educated, urbane and sophisticated expatriate city people flooding into rural backwaters sometimes felt unreal, but since it was happening it was certainly real enough. But at times it felt uncomfortable to be part of it because of the escapist aspect to this movement and the romanticized notions of country life.

Occasionally it would seem that we were living out a dream, other times a nightmare. A friend woke up one morning to find his beautiful poet-philosopher wife gone and a note under the aloe plant saying she had "fallen out of love." He said next time he was going to look for a woman who "likes country and western music and knows how to take care of a dog."

But people seeking to escape on the Leelanau were not alone. In the eighties it was as if the entire country wanted to escape and had gone to bed with a head cold, taking along a stack of movie magazines and a box of bonbons. We regressed. We were a nation in retrograde.

We escaped in different ways, but we escaped. Some of us became born-again Christians and followers of Jim and Tammy Faye Bakker. Some of us, like Shirley MacLaine, sought out psychic healers and so-called spiritual leaders in the occult realm, channelers of "Seth," and dolphins. We all focused on food. We discovered orange roughy and Alaskan char and basil pesto and cilantro and blue corn tortilla chips. There was no escaping the escapists.

In *Answered Prayers* Truman Capote writes of the expatriate Americans in Paris, "Very gradually I was absorbed into this squalid caravan. . . ." I felt that way sometimes, and not just about the squalid caravan I was in. It was as if I suddenly looked around and saw myself under an enormous patchwork quilt of the continental forty-eight states, and a lot of other Americans were there too—all of us down with the flu, eating and watching late night movies on TV. But I take a charitable view of myself and my friends and everybody else too. We *needed* to escape, many of us, because the problems confronting us—the nuclear threat, the global warming trend, the huge numbers of children in poverty, the homeless, AIDS—were so vast, so awful, and so overwhelming that the reasonable response was to try to put them out of our minds and seek a little immediate relief and concentrate on projects we could accomplish, like getting wood for the winter or planting a garden. As for trying to attract "positive energy" with Austrian crystals, well, as the old woman said, "If it can't help, it can't hurt."

I happen to think now that the problems were not so insurmountable, *are* not so insurmountable; but I can think that now that I've sat on the bench for several innings.

Faith Popcorn, a Madison Avenue marketing analyst quoted

in the *Detroit News* in February, 1988, predicted that the 1990s will be "the fifties revisited" because "people are homesick for human warmth and community. They are tired of wallowing in a morass of nothingness." Yes, of course. But people were homesick for human warmth and community in the 1980s too. And we had a fifties revival in the 1980s, but human warmth and community are easier said than done; they cannot be created with red and black buffalo plaid wool shirts and stores selling Mom's chocolate chip cookies, or even by more labor intensive efforts such as building your own log home or doing organic gardening. I think we've seen the fifties revival in the eighties, and that what we will see in the nineties will be the nineties—people ready to take hold and dig in and come to grips with reality. You can only escape so long before the bed becomes heaped with old Kleenexes and old candy wrappers and old movie magazines you've read already. We're done with revival; we're ready for renewal.

Michiko Kakutani, reviewing Jane Smiley's novel, *Ordinary Love and Good Will* for the *New York Times* on October 3, 1989, quotes one of Smiley's characters from an earlier novella, who talks of being initiated into *the age of grief.* "It is a rite of passage," Kakutani writes, "that has to do not only with awareness of mortality, but also with the realization that love ends, that families come apart, that even parents cannot protect their children from the consequences of change and loss. It is the realization that the barriers between the circumstances of oneself and the rest of the world have broken down. . . ." I think that is the point we've reached, or will soon reach, as a nation: the age of grief. Also the age of awareness.

We are in a state of transition, a state of change, not only in our families, as in the novel Kakutani reviews, but in our communities as well. Madeleine L'Engle, a writer perhaps best known for her children's books such as *A Wrinkle in Time* and *A Swiftly Tilting Planet,* books I would characterize as religious mysticism for children, tends to take the long view as a perceiver of the human scene: she says this kind of change is the normal reaction to stasis, or un-change. In an excerpt from one of her journals, *A Circle of Quiet,* she makes the following observation: "Because we are human, our communities tend to become rigid. They stop evolving, revolving, which is essential to their life, as is the revolution of the earth about the sun essential to the life of our planet, our full family and basic establishment. Hence, we must constantly be in a state of revolution or we die."

So people experiment, seek change, go too far, exhaust themselves, return to basics, get sick and require bed rest or escape, regress and have a fifties revival and find that old formulas don't apply to new conditions, and seek change, and return to old ways, again and again, in a seesawing dialectic that characterizes the human condition down through the ages.

We are in a constant state of evolution, I like to think, as opposed to revolution, or in addition to it, only in recent times it seems we have been evolving more culturally and personally, rather than biologically or politically. Yes, sometimes it is a squalid caravan, and I am in it, and I don't mind. Sometimes it is also a seeking for the Holy Grail, and no matter how deluded the quest, it has its shining moments. Karlfried Graf Von Durckheim, in an article excerpted in *Parabola* entitled "Healing Power and Gesture," writes "Life, being a moving process, does not tolerate anything static."

Or, as Heraclitus said in 500 B.C., "You never step into the river in the same place twice." So my place in the river was the Leelanau Peninsula in the 1980s, or at least that was one place in one river that I happened to be able to write about.

I think I know what attracts people to life on this peninsula and makes them want to read about it, because I know what brought me back. I wanted to live again in a place where people knew each other, have known each other for years, and where, if you say, "Remember when . . . ?" they do.

It is hard to live our lives in places where we have no memories. It limits the depth of our relationships—not just to people, but to places, to seasons. On the simplest level, knowing how this fall differs from last fall deepens my awareness. If anybody else in my community, or several anybodies, has a different or similar awareness, this also broadens my perception, makes it more prismatic, more real.

In *Silas Marner,* George Eliot writes—in 1861—

Even people whose lives have been made various by learning sometimes find it hard to keep a fast hold on their habitual views of life, on their faith in the Invisible—nay, on the sense that their past joys and sorrows are a real experience, when they are suddenly transported to a new land, where the beings around them know nothing of their history, and share none of their ideas—where their mother earth shows another lap, and human life has other forms than those on which their souls have been nourished. Minds that have been unhinged from their old faith and love have perhaps sought this Lethean influence of exile, in which the past becomes dreamy because its symbols have all vanished, and the present, too, is dreamy because it is linked with no memories.

To all the flying Silas Marners in America today, the regional writing of a Garrison Keillor or an Annie Dillard offers a context, a centering. There must be a memory in the blood for the way, for instance, a blaze of sumac on a fall day makes you feel sad and tingly at the same time and like finding a lover quick before winter sets in. Or the way the WONKA, WONKA, WONKA of the geese overhead makes you want to get the wood stacked. It seems that geese and sumac, in their myriad forms, are some of our only remaining uncontrived feedback in an increasingly weird world.

In this view, regional writing is not merely providing people with a way to escape from the real world, it *is* the real world. It is the place of reference from which we can assess the rest of what's going on. It has a long history in this country, at least as far back as Thoreau, and it's as valid today as it was then, perhaps more so.

Contents

Close to the Village

Village Life

ANYONE WHO HAS ever walked around a small village at suppertime on a spring night and heard the sounds of children playing in the park and the choir practicing in the church and watched the mist rising from the lake and heard the redwing blackbirds calling to their mates will know what I mean when I say there is something about village life that calls out to one, that makes one know that down through the ages we have all lived in villages and there's a gene for village life in most of us.

Although village life is by its very nature life writ small, life lived on a Currier and Ives plate, and can be cloying and claustrophobic at times, there are other times when the very sweetness, simplicity, and peacefulness to be found there are some of the rare, lovely things we are offered in this life.

A few years ago, in the late summer of 1982, I moved with my family to the outskirts of the village of Lake Leelanau, close enough to the woods to hear the owls hoot at night and close enough to the village to hear the Angelus ring at noon.

We had lived in Traverse City, a town of about sixteen thousand—small by most people's standards, but I had grown up in an even smaller town, Glen Arbor on the Leelanau Peninsula, and wanted to show my children what small-town life was like, and be again in a place where I knew all the people and they knew me and people talked to each other in grocery store lines and at the post office. Such a place is Lake Leelanau, a village of about a hundred and fifty people, small enough to give one a sense of one's self and a sense of the whole and a sense of one's place in it all.

To live in a small town in the hinterlands is to know that there still exists in rural America a heartland beyond the confines of cities and TV, a place in the mind and in reality that is a generative force in this country's sense of itself. It's the reason politicians campaign in East Junction; they know that there among the lilacs and the apple blossoms in the high school gym they will appear to TV viewers to be standing at the center of democracy. Democracy is rural, if you think about it. Democracy is rural because in small communities it's still possible for people to know the issues, and each other.

At its best, Lake Leelanau gives me a primal sense of the human community, a sharing of life with those who acknowledge—albeit silently, simply by their being there too—that we cannot live ontologically meaningful lives in isolation.

Sometimes when I've been away from the village for a few days or a few hours and drive the last twenty hilly miles up the Leelanau Peninsula and down into the valley around Lake Leelanau, I feel what I can only imagine all people have always felt when they see the hills of home—the hunter home from a week of hunting mastodons, the waitress home from the night shift in the diner—that sense of coming into one's own village, where the smoke from the neighbors' chimneys is inexplicably reassuring.

The other day when I drove through the village—after a windy night that rocked our old farmhouse and rattled the wind chime until I dreamed I was in China, a wild wind that knocked down limbs all along the highway—I noticed a homemade sign in the Houdek's yard announcing the birth—the night before—of a daughter. "Polka Princess," the sign said. Some people may care when Lady Di has a baby, but I care when the Houdeks do. Or the Parsons, who six months before had tied three balloons to their mailbox announcing the birth of a baby girl. My spirits lifted, seeing those three pink balloons, and still do when I think of it.

Things happen in a village where you know people and see

the same people every day that don't happen, I don't think, in a place where you don't. The other day my daughter got new pink tights at the store and on the way home insisted on stopping and showing them to the postmistress, Marie Hope. Now Marie Hope, called Aunt Marie by half the people who pick up their mail here, is a special kind of person, the kind of person you could show your new pink tights to, if you happened to have some, and who would be just as excited for you as you were for yourself. Nonetheless, all other things being equal, I don't think if Marie were a postmistress in Manhattan, my daughter would be showing her her new pink tights.

Marie Hope is one of my personal candidates for sainthood. A tall, dignified, white-haired, pretty woman in her sixth or seventh decade of life, she listens to and cares for more people every day in this small town than most psychiatrists do in a lifetime. I have seen her endlessly look at trip pictures and wedding pictures and hear about who got born and who got married and who fell ill, and I'm always astonished at her genuine interest, her calm and wise compassion.

Marie (Plamondon) Hope grew up in Lake Leelanau and has been postmistress here most of her life. She's been postmistress in two or three different buildings around town. She was postmistress in a building up on Meinard Street that's now the County Social Services thrift shop. She was postmistress in an old cinder-block building in the center of town when the post office was combined with the phone company. She says people used to call up and ask her to read their mail to them over the phone. She would politely explain that she couldn't legally do that, but she would tell them if they'd gotten a letter so they could know whether or not to make the trip to the post office.

One day a year or two ago Marie says she got a call from a woman who used to live in Lake Leelanau years before, a retarded girl Marie had gone to school with at Lake Leelanau St. Mary's. "The kids made fun of her, called her Martha Bum," Marie says. "I'd always felt sorry for her. She wanted me to go buy some flowers and put them on her folks' grave up in the cemetery, so I did. Another time she called just to talk. It was one of those calls, I couldn't figure out who it was at first. I said, 'You're lonely, aren't you, Martha?' and she said yes, she was lonely. Another time I got a call from one of the women in the house where she lived in San Francisco and the girl said Martha had had a fall and was in the hospital and would I write to her, so of course I did." I picture Marie going up the hill to put flowers on the grave and picture her as a child walking down the dirt streets to the school. Compassion for others must have been born early in her, but it has to have been deepened and expanded by her years as postmistress, friend, and neighbor to the people in this small village.

Margaret Skeba is the postmistress's assistant in Lake Leelanau. She is new to the post office and to the ways of the post office. She was a housewife for years until her husband had a stroke. She is a wonderful woman, but quite different from Marie. When Marie isn't there, she listens to polka music on a portable radio. She likes to mop the floor after people track mud across it and keeps the bucket and mop ready.

One day Margaret said to me, "The nuns always told me the two best things about me were my name, Margaret, and my eyebrows. They showed me how to keep them nice." She then demonstrated by wetting an index finger on her tongue and wiping one eyebrow neatly in one direction and the other eyebrow just as neatly in the other, "like that." Later her niece Paulette said, "Aunt Margaret is a card."

The post office is a focal point of social life in Lake Leelanau. This is where I often run into Ted Grant, who always says, "I'm all right, it's the world that's wrong," as he gets his mail in this post office that he owns and rents and that is in his backyard. "You must be Pat Stockin's girl," he said to me one day shortly after I'd moved to the village. "I can see that Pat Stockin's in your face." I am not offended by this, but amused: I also figure out who people are on this small peninsula by figuring out who they look like.

When everyone is related and interrelated, and lives overlap over and over again, and each family has its share of slow thinkers and eccentric geniuses, its ne'er-do-wells and brilliant achievers, the expression, "There but for the grace of God go I," takes on literal as well as metaphorical meaning. People who live in small towns and have daily awareness of this seem to have an increased tolerance of each other, making small towns cheerful and amusing places to inhabit. And Ted Grant is one of the foremost proponents of good cheer and tolerance.

Ted's 1940s-style brick bungalow is about two hundred feet from the back of the post office; in the summer I often wave to him as he cultivates his roses, and in the winter I sometimes see him filling his various bird feeders. You have to picture Ted Grant. He's a barrel-chested, outgoing man in his mid-seventies, a widower, a tireless worker. He ran the town's gas station for years, working fifteen hours a day seven days a week. He says his work habits were honed by farm labor as a kid and by jobs like the one he had during the Depression, cutting and splitting cord wood for two dollars a day.

His house fronts on the Lake Leelanau "narrows," where the lake's natural wasp waist creates a marshy estuary more river than lake. One day in the early spring Ted said to me in the post office, "You oughta come down some morning and see the ducks come in when I call 'em." I imagined he was a professional duck caller, the kind they profile in men's sporting magazines. Hoping to hear him do it right there in the P.O., I asked him how he did it. "I call 'em," he says, "'here duckie, here duckie, here duckie.'"

Ted Grant can be seen a couple of times a week during the spring and summer out tending to saplings he's planted along the highway. He rides a big tractor, pulling barrels of water and mulch behind him on a flat rig, and he always waves. At seventy-six, he says he's mainly interested in the survival of two dozen young trees. I asked him about it one day in the post office and he said, "In twenty-five, fifty years, I'd like people to have these big trees out there and maybe say," he chuckles, "'Ted Grant, he really took care of those trees.'"

Our village of Lake Leelanau is not a pretentious village, I like to think, but a down-home village. It has escaped the gentrification that some of the peninsula's tonier, shoreside, Lake

Michigan villages have fallen prey to, and therefore it has re-
tained its authenticity.

A few nights ago when I was getting my car fixed at Ted's—
the Standard Station that still bears Ted Grant's name—I took
my four-year-old daughter and walked around the village. It
was one of those beautiful spring evenings when it feels as if
everything, including one's self, has a helium lift to it: water
running in the ditches, sky a pale blue, leaves curled tight to
unfurl at a moment's notice, balm of Gilead scenting the air. It
is hard to be sad in the spring in such weather. The challenge is
to be as eager for renewal as everything else—frogs, ducks,
birds, bunnies—but not as reckless.

The village is small. From the hill behind my house I can see
the whole thing. There's an old school in the village and a
grocery store; a Catholic church and an abandoned cobblestone
convent; a pizza place that rents cross-country skis, a furniture
store that rents videos, and a hardware store that takes packages
for UPS; two bars (Dick's Pour House and Dan's Power
House); a thrift shop and an antique store; Ted's Standard Station; and a doctor's office. There's a small park called The
Grove and a few pleasantly random streets: St. Mary's, St.
Joseph's, Meinard, Phillips, and Main. There are some comfortable, old wood-frame houses and a few classic Michigan cobblestone homes. Ted Grant said when he was a kid they used
horses to haul the stones out of the bay and that even today
those stones will sweat on a hot day.

The village of Lake Leelanau is on low hills above the lake.
Today the afternoon sky above the town is dramatically ter-
raced with orange and cerise clouds, coming to a vee like geese
over the western hills.

In the Penny Power Thrift Shop up on Meinard the elderly
women who volunteer to run it are sorting and pricing old
clothes. One woman has white hair, a second is wearing a knit
hat, and a third is in tweed slacks.

"I forget where I read it, but something's going to happen
in five, seven, or ten years," says the woman in tweed slacks.

"It says in the Bible," says the woman in the knit hat, "we are living in historical times. We are going to see Armageddon."

"Now you take Reagan," says the woman with the white hair. "He's a born-again Christian. I'll bet if you could get him to sit down and talk to you, really talk to you, you know, an honest conversation that wasn't going to be reported, just the two of you, one-on-one, and you were to ask him why he sent those boys into Grenada, he'd say he didn't know why, it was *the Lord* guiding him."

"What is this Armageddon?" asks the woman in tweed slacks.

"It's destruction beyond destruction," says the authoritative woman in the knit hat. "I could bring you a book on it, but you probably wouldn't read it. I'll send it to someone in prison."

Back out on Main Street, Nick Lederle is coming across the street toward N.J.'s grocery store. Nick is a retired oil company attorney who spent years in the Mideast and speaks fluent Arabic. He grew up here. He is known locally for eloquent speech and for sometimes dressing up in loden green jodhpurs, a loden green hunter's jacket, and a loden green hunter's hat with the beard of a mountain stag sticking up on one side like a small elegant whisk broom.

I sometimes try to picture him as he must have appeared in the oil fields of Arabia, dressed in his own distinctive garb, matching wits with the sheiks.

Mild eccentricity garners a person elbowroom in the close quarters of a small village, and Nick and I have that cultivated eccentricity in common. It's something you learn early in a small town, and the wonder of it is that people not only tolerate us more than they might in a larger urban setting but love us more too. We are their spice of life, and they wouldn't give us up for anything.

Nick and his wife take care of the tubs of geraniums that decorate the town. His wife, Elsie, is a gracious woman and an excellent conversationalist. She owned and ran one of the town's taverns for years. "Elsie didn't run a bar," Nick says.

"She had a club, an intellectual and spiritual oasis. She catered to people."

My daughter and I go into N.J.'s for a pop. This store, always in the Plamondon family, is now run by Wayne Plamondon and his wife and sons. The meat counter is a town gathering place, a place where the photos of new babies appear pasted above the bologna, a place where photos of fish caught out of Lake Leelanau also appear, the counter a picture yardstick of the quotidian rhythms of the village.

Proust said in *The Sweet Cheat Gone,* "The bonds that unite another person to oneself exist only in our mind. Memory as it grows fainter relaxes them and notwithstanding the illusion by which we would fain be cheated and with which out of love, friendship, politeness, deference, duty, we cheat other people, we exist alone."

In the metaphysical or philosophical sense that Proust was talking about, we are alone, in that we're born into this world alone and we leave it alone. But there's a difference between being alone and being lonely—isolated, alienated, and out of touch.

The constant contact with others in a small village, the daily awareness of the warp, weft, and weave of their lives, is some of our most sensible feedback in an increasingly insensible world, and it keeps that terrible sense of estrangement at bay, even while it confirms our essential uniqueness and difference from others. I think that's what makes Marie Hope one of the most sound-minded people I know; her position at one of the centers of this small hub of humanity keeps her grounded in reality and merciful in her judgments.

Over the bridge in Lake Leelanau is the house of Molly and Fred Petroskey. Molly and Fred have recently come back to this village after years in Boston, where Fred, a successful portrait painter, taught art and Molly taught fifth-grade science. "We have a place on Martha's Vineyard," Molly says. "We haven't been back there in three years." Still in their fifties, the Petroskeys took an early retirement so Fred could paint.

"This country is not just a peninsula," Molly says, "it's more like an island. We spent a lot of time on Martha's Vineyard and there are a lot of similarities. Family is very important."

"I walked into the post office when I came back," Fred says, "and there was Marie Hope, and she'd been there when I'd left at eighteen. And she said, 'Oh, hi, Fred,' as if only a week had gone by."

Fred's mother was born a Plamondon, as was Marie Hope. When I ask Fred how they are related he laughs and says, "This is how we spend our Sunday afternoons since we've come back, trying to figure out who is related to whom and how you figure a sixth cousin twice removed. It's Trivial Pursuit, but you have to have been born here to play it."

Molly says she and Fred knew each other at Lake Leelanau St. Mary's, the Catholic school in the village; they didn't start dating until Molly was a senior and Fred came home on vacation from the University of Detroit and the nuns drafted him into directing the senior play. Fred asked Molly to the 1954 prom and they've been together ever since.

"You complicate your life by living where everyone knows you," Fred says. "You have to go to their funerals, their weddings, their birthdays and chicken barbecues. But they have to go to yours too."

Molly says she and Fred could have bought land on Lake Michigan and built a new house, but they decided to buy an old farmhouse at the edge of the village and restore it. They wanted to make a commitment to the village they'd grown up in. "People were telling us about retirement in Ashville, North Carolina," Fred says, "and I thought, 'I know a place as nice as that.' I looked at it this way; would I rather die in Ashville, North Carolina, where no one knew me or would I rather be here?" He laughs. "Here I'm related to everybody."

Back across the bridge, past the marsh and the frog symphony, on the way to the park, I run into Huston Cradduck. He is the town woodcutter and lives in a large hill house at the corner of St. Joseph's and Meinard Streets. Huston is the resident expert on purple martins. He calls them blue martins. Huston has a Southern accent and a Southern way of talking that is wonderful to listen to.

"Those blue martins," he says, "they get up 'fore crack day. They eat more mosquitoes in a day than what they themselves weigh, if you can believe it.

"Blue martins send their scouts up about the tenth of May," he says, "then they come with their families. They like a clean house, seven inches every way, and a two-inch hole. And another thing on the blue martin, he likes wide open spaces, clear sailin'. They don't like no red for their house—they'll scream and holler. Black is too hot for their babies. Two of their favorite colors is green and white. They're sumpin' to watch. They teach their babies how to fly.

"At one time, here," he says, "I had forty families of blue martins round about the house. I could sit on my porch in the evenin's in my shirtsleeves and never get even one mosquito bite."

Walking around a village is a lot like reading a newspaper, only not as depressing. You get to feel the real sense of what's going on—the pink tights and purple martins and new babies as well as Armageddon. You get to feel yourself in the web of life. When you get back home you can say, "Well, that's what people are like. That's reality out there," reassured for another day that nothing has changed much about basic humanity.

Bean's Birthday

WHEN MR. ROGERS sings, "These are the people in your neighborhood, in your neighborhood . . ." this is the prelude to a little visit to the postman or the clerk at the grocery store. He never sings, "These are the people in your neighborhood," and then takes you to visit someone handicapped.

In the minds of most of us, handicapped people are not part of our neighborhoods, not because they aren't there but because we don't know how to relate to them. We believe that these people are institutionalized or put in foster care; we don't have daily dealings with them, not in the way that humans since the beginning of time would have, and we're probably all missing some essential part of our human perspective because of this.

This whole issue was brought home to me a couple of years ago when my neighbor Linda invited me to a birthday party for her neighbor. "I'm having a birthday party for Bean," she said. "He lives just across the field and up the hill." I asked what I could bring. "Oh, just a card," she said, "but nothing too sophisticated. Bean's retarded."

Linda lives about a mile from me on County Road 645, in a yellow farmhouse nestled in a valley. A small creek runs by the front door so people use the back door. This is the way we came in for Bean's birthday party—past the washing machine, pop bottles, and kids' coats. There were about five of us ladies from the surrounding hills there and Linda's four children. Linda's husband was at work at his bar, "The Hard Times

Saloon," in Empire at the other end of the peninsula. It was midday.

Never having met Bean before I was surprised to find that he was an older man and this was his fifty-first birthday. I had always imagined retarded people as being younger. This was the first of a series of small shocks I had about my own ignorance. Obviously retarded people could be any age; it was my experience that was limited.

The other ladies gave Bean coloring books and small toy cars. I wished I had thought to give him something besides a card. Bean was excited and happy. He ate a big piece of cake.

Later Linda said she had wanted to give Bean a birthday party because he'd never had one. "He has a mental age of about five," she said. "For me it was like seeing any five-year-old kid who'd never had a birthday party."

Linda has also taken Bean trick-or-treating on Halloween. "Some people are surprised," she says, "when they come to the door and see him with our kids. They say to him, 'Aren't you too old to be trick-or-treating?' I'll say, Yes, but he enjoys it." She takes him to McDonald's, a favorite outing. Sometimes her husband, Bob, takes Bean with him to the bar. "Not all day," Linda says, "but for a couple of hours. Bean loves it."

Bean's given name is Albion. He is now fifty-three. He lives with an older brother and sister. The older brother supports Bean and the sister. The sister does the cooking and cleaning. Bean has never been institutionalized. The sister's version of how he came to be retarded is that her mother was on the phone, pregnant with Bean, and lightning struck the phone. I remark to Linda that it's nice of Bean's brother to take care of him and Linda says, "I don't think he ever thought of *not* doing it." Later when I talk to the brother, an accomplished housepainter who works for wealthy Lelanders, he says, "Well, when my mom died, I took over. It hasn't always been easy. It hasn't been that hard either."

Linda is an unusual person in that she has a knack for seeing potential and building self-esteem in others. When she first met Bean seven years ago he talked very little, she says. "Blue car," "red car," and "you fifty?" were about the extent of his conversation. One day some people were visiting Linda and asked Bean his name. He wouldn't or couldn't say it. Linda said, "I'll give you a piece of pizza if you say your name." A minute later he said, "Bean?" Linda says now, "It was like he'd never said it before."

"Bean is eager to please," Linda says. "The first thing he does when he comes over is take out the garbage. I'll say, 'Bean, you take out the garbage better than anyone I know,' and he's just so thrilled with that."

Linda is a mother and a day-care mother. "Seeing Bean," she says, "it was just like seeing another kid. If he likes coloring books, that's what he should have. We got him a child's tape recorder for Christmas. He loves it. I'd like to be able to teach him to write his ABCs, but I don't have the brains for it, I guess, because I haven't been able to do it. I'd like to see him go to a special school in Traverse City."

Linda has opened the way for other neighbors in their relationship with Bean. He now takes mail (from the mailboxes at the road up or down long hilly driveways) to two neighbors. He stacked ten cords of wood for another neighbor and received gifts as compensation. He does not visit regularly with other neighborhood families as he does with Linda's, but he is viewed as a part of the community. "I don't think of Bean as retarded now," one neighbor lady said, "he's just Bean."

Making Wood

I HEAT WITH WOOD. Most of us up here do. Wood is still cheaper than any other fuel, and it's available. Some of us cut our own wood, but to do that you have to have a woodlot, a truck, a saw in good condition, and time. My husband and I cut our own wood one winter, but in retrospect it seems like that's *all* we did.

So now we buy our wood from woodcutters. Over the years I have come in contact with a number of woodcutters and can say without reservation that they are the most independent-minded people I have ever known. The reason for this seems to be that woodcutting attracts them, being perhaps the last profession in the world a man can do alone—all alone—with just a truck and a chain saw.

Huston Cradduck, the woodcutter, has a wooding yard in an old gravel pit about a half mile down the slope from us. Sometimes early in the morning in the fall we can hear him down there, thunking wood into the back of his pickup truck, filling orders for the season's late buyers. Sometimes when I drive to the post office to get my mail, I can see him out there with his yellow tape measure, measuring off an exact cord for a customer.

One day I went along with him as he worked, so I could see what it was like, cutting wood for a living. We began the day in the gravel pit at 8:00 A.M. Huston, a young Indian man named Dale Miller, and an old man called Bouncer are working a mechanical wood splitter.

The sound of the wood splitter in the old gravel pit is high and whiny, like a cicada. It drowns out everything, even thought. Finally the wood splitter stops. For a minute the sound seems to still ring in the gravel pit, in the rock I'm leaning against.

"How's that for making wood?" Huston asks. He lights up one of his Odin cigars. He seems pleased with himself. I ask him to explain the expression "making wood." "It's certainly wood when it's a tree," he says, "but then when you go performin' it over, that's called making wood."

We climb into the cab of his old red pickup truck, Huston, Dale Miller, and me. Bouncer goes back to his trailer at the top of the gravel pit. We drive about a mile down M-204, past my house and a couple of other farmhouses to a deep, rutted two-track that bumps along through a swamp. The cab of the truck smells of a rich blend of gasoline and Odin cigars, and every time we go over a bump, a little puff of that odor bounces up with us.

"When I first come to this country," Huston says, "I bought me a forty-acre parcel in here, put up a cabin for my wife and kids. When I first come to this country, I had twenty-five dollars to my name." I ask Huston what country he's from. "Missouri," he says, "Missouri."

Huston Cradduck was born in the little town of Rudy, Arkansas, in 1921. "I got to fourth grade, then I was workin' in the woods, skiddin' ties with a mule." It was the height of the Depression; he didn't return to school. He began cutting cord wood with a crosscut saw when he was ten. "Back them days, that was fifty cents a cord."

He figures that when he was younger he could cut, split, and load ten cords in an eight-hour day. A cord of wood weighs, "in the estimate neighborhood," about fifteen hundred pounds. "That's a young man's day," he says. Now at sixty-seven he only works a six-hour day. Huston and his wife live in one of the biggest and best-kept houses in the village. They've been married forty-seven years. "Won't be long and it'll be a Golden Wedding."

The truck begins to climb up out of the swamp and into the hills. Finally, Huston pulls to a stop near the ridge. He gets out and oils his chain saw and then begins to "slice down" several beech and maple trees marked with blue paint for culling. Huston is a tall, skinny man with ropey muscles; he clambers up and down the steep hills, as he says, "like a billy goat." Dale Miller climbs up and down the hills too, hauling logs to the pickup truck, and appears to do so without exertion.

Huston tells me to stay clear of where they're cutting. Has he ever had any accidents in the woods? "I lost five teeth once. I worked 'til quittin' time that afternoon, then went to the dentist and had 'em pulled. A limb I was cuttin' snapped back and hit me in the face." Another time, on North Manitou, a limb "sliced" his head; he had to wait several hours for the mail boat to take him to the hospital in Northport to get "sewed up." That day he did not work until quitting time, but he was back on the job two days later.

I find a place to sit on a large, blue-gray rock well up the hill. It is mid-morning now, but the deep woods are still surprisingly cool. From far away I hear a thrush sing. I have brought along a copy of the *Detroit News*, but I don't feel like reading it. It sits beside me on the ground, the faces of presidential candidates staring up at me from the ferns. Not until I look at the date on the newspaper do I realize it's the Fourth of July.

When the men take a break, we talk about the wooding business. Huston gets thirty-five dollars a face cord. "It seems like a lot of money," he says, "but not by the time you figure your truck, your saw, your wood splitter, your gas, your oil, your repairs. Then I gotta give John Simpson (the man on whose land he's cutting) every fourth cord." Huston says it takes about an hour to cut a cord of wood. It takes another hour to load, haul, and unload it; this process is repeated again when the wood is delivered to the customer. Huston laughs. "One woman said to me, 'Now my husband wants you to stack it right there between those two trees.' I said, 'No, ma'am, that's *his* job.'"

Sitting there listening, I am thinking of a *New Yorker* cartoon some months back that showed a bunch of city folk all walking around the city with their matching canvas wood carriers filled with Georgia fatwood. I am thinking that there is a lot that people don't know about cutting and burning wood. We burn twenty cords a winter, and sometime in February—after months of cleaning up the tracked-in woodchips and snow, after months of getting up at 3:00 A.M. to bank the fire—I would gladly trade my wood stove for a furnace or a servant.

"My wife says I'm crazy," Huston says. "There ain't hardly no money in it, but I'll tell you, I *like* the woods, and I *don't like* no four walls. Then I had a little bit of trouble, takin' orders offa anybody. One time a man cussed me and used my name. I was layin' blocks and I was about to lay one upside his head. I said, 'Man, just 'cause you're the boss, you ain't go no right to cuss me, all you do is pay me, man, you're human same as me.'" He pauses a minute, then says, "Me and my wife got a nice house in town, got a dollar to spend if we want one, got three kids grown and married off." He stubs out his cigar and picks up his chain saw, "I don't need nobody tellin' me how to live, that's all, don't need nobody tellin' me when I *can* and when I *cain't*."

November, Season of Ghost Suppers

I HAD NOT KNOWN MY Indian husband long when he invited me to join him in a Native American custom called Ghost Suppers. Ghost Suppers, for the uninitiated, are a traditional celebration that precedes Thanksgiving and coincides with Halloween and partakes of elements of both. It is a time of feasting that commemorates the spirits of those who have gone before. The people feasting both symbolically represent the people of the past and eucharistically honor them.

On the particular November night when I went to my first Ghost Supper, a light cold rain—not unpleasant—was blowing in off Lake Michigan and through the small Indian village of Peshawbestown.

We walked through the mist from house to house, each well-lighted and warm inside. We would eat food that was like a Thanksgiving feast—turkey, venison, cornbread, gravy, pies, mashed potatoes, squash—and then move back out into the cold again.

Other groups would pass us along the road, some with heads jacket-shrouded against the rain. There was a feeling of camaraderie, of people happy in the dark.

My husband told me as we walked along that when he was growing up in Harbor Springs, his parents would set the table late at night with a full meal like the kind we were eating. Later, neighborhood children would come in and silently eat. He thought his parents, converts to Catholicism, had some ambivalence about the custom, as he and his four sisters did not participate.

Today the Catholic Church in Peshawbestown and in several other Indian communities has combined the festival of Ghost Suppers with the church holiday of All Saints' Day, November 1. I have been to a few of these church potlucks and they are nice gatherings—usually held in the afternoon on the Saturday or Sunday closest to November 1. But somehow they have lacked the magic of that first Ghost Supper, the intriguing friendly quietness of Indian people going through the cold mist from house to house, the wonderful contrast of the cold, dark November rain outside and the warmth and light and food inside.

Memories of that first Ghost Supper came back the other day when I ran into my friend Suzanne in the grocery store and asked her what she was doing for Thanksgiving. What Suzanne was doing for Thanksgiving would daunt a lesser soul. She was having her two ex-husbands, their girlfriends, one ex-mother-in-law, her present husband, and various children and friends from all relationships for dinner. "We want the kids to know we're friends," she said.

Suzanne is a beautiful person—not only in the sense that *People* magazine might mean it, but also in the sense that St. Francis of Assisi might mean it. She is gifted with a generous and forgiving nature that those of us who can't even speak to our ex-husbands on the phone, let alone their mothers, can only stand in awe of. She, like myself, is a member of what journalists and demographers like to call the post-World-War-II-baby-boom-generation (one key on the computer). This is the generation of which Tom McGuane has said, "We tried a lot of things. A lot of things didn't work, but we tried a lot of things."

Suzanne lives on the harbor in the fishing village of Leland, in among the fishing boats, crimson sunsets, and winter storms, in a house like the one Cher lived in in *The Witches of Eastwick.* She reminds me of Cher, too: honest, blessed with movie-star good-looks, the kind of person who if the earth flooded tomorrow you'd expect to pop to the surface a week later in a homemade raft. Because she has an unerring sense for what's fair and right and proper, Suzanne has come up with her own version of a Ghost Supper. For a Ghost Supper is not necessarily for your friends or necessarily for your enemies; it's a ceremony to show respect for the past, for that which has gone before, "so the kids can know we're friends." The idea is that, with the past acknowledged, one can get on with the present.

Other cultures have had, or do have, autumn ceremonies similar to Suzanne's Thanksgiving or the Native American Ghost Suppers. A local herbalist, Lori Cruden, tells me that in former times the Celts celebrated Halloween as a religious ritual. "This was the time of the Weaponless Warrior," she says, "a time when the veil between the two worlds, the mundane world and the spirit world, was the most thin." Perhaps it's the old Celt in me, perhaps it's the autumn mists on this peninsula, but fall does seem to be a time when the spirits of the past are abroad, a time of reflection, of mental drawer-cleaning.

Psychiatrist Alan McGlashan in his book *The Savage and Beautiful Country* says, "Since man must remember if he is not to become meaningless, and must forget if he is not to go mad, what shall he do?" He recommends taking a second look at the customs of the past, "for the essence of this earthly wisdom lies precisely in its slow, centuried synthesis of thinking with feeling. . . . It would be well if man could recapture this richer, older mode of response to the enigma of existence. . . . What is needed is an extension of contemporary consciousness to include what can be defined as the translucent quality of all things. . . . This, once caught, even for a moment, transforms the sensible universe, investing all objects with a sharp intensity of being."

Not just members of the loosely confederated baby-boom generation in America—largely suburban, largely rootless, largely raised on Cheerios and TV—but also newcomers to this country need to formulate some ceremonies to deal with the past so we don't end up living in a vacuum. I'm thinking here

of Mad Sao, a character in Maxine Hong Kingston's *China Men,* a book about Chinese immigrants to California. Mad Sao did well in the new world and made money and had a wife and a house with a mortgage. But the mother he'd left behind haunted his dreams with her tales of death by starvation. Not until Mad Sao went back to China and ate and drank on her grave, ceremonially, did his mother's spirit leave him in peace.

In those ancient countries we all come from—England, China, and Michigan when it was young—there were ancient customs we associate with "primitive" man, with our primitive selves. In fact those primitive antecedents might have been more sophisticated than our present-day customs, for they succeeded, where ours often do not, in being emotionally satisfying and in linking us to each other and to what McGlashan calls "the enigma of existence." Who in our society hasn't felt vaguely bereft of a culture after watching the Macy's Thanksgiving Day Parade? Or after celebrating Christmas even though one isn't really a Christian or hasn't been inside a church in years?

"It seems that what is genuine in our need to solemnify, celebrate and ritualize the things that happen in our lives, originates in something as basic as the incompleteness of our being," writes D. M. Dooling, founder and publisher of the metaphysical magazine *Parabola,* "for we see that a person or a community usually seeks a ceremony at the moment of recognizing human inadequacy in the face of life events. The ceremony is a reminder of our possible relation with the sacred and no ceremony can do more than help the celebrant to remember himself in all his possible dimensions."

The respect for the past represented by the ceremonial Ghost Suppers is at bottom a regard for history. History, accurately recalled, keeps us honest. Anne Herbert, writing in her fictitious *Rising Sun Neighborhood Newsletter,* runs the following announcement: "Dr. Weaver will be teaching a history class in the basement of St. John's United Methodist Church for people old enough to have seen an important part of their lives forgotten. Dr. Weaver says, 'It's a mistake to try to teach history to teenagers. You can't really get interested in remembering and analyzing the past until something you thought would last a long time is over.'"

I don't know at what exact moment—after what Neolithic divorce, death, miscarriage, war, or falling out—some tribal elder, wise in the ways of the world and the human psyche, suggested the first ceremonial Halloween, Ghost Supper, or lunch on Mama's grave. What ancestor in bearskins intuited this trick for healing the human heart? I know it works. I know that that November night when I entered those houses "as a spirit" and was served a meal by people who didn't acknowledge my presence except "as a spirit," there was something wonderfully accepting, as if I'd united with and transcended the past, been offered a moment of divine grace and redemption, of connection to the larger human community and to the mystery of existence.

So that's why today I've invited some friends in and I'm

spending the day cooking, my kitchen filled with the sounds of Verdi and the smell of roasting turkey. Outside the hills are autumn purple, their flanks undulating under moving clouds. The wind smells like snow, although there's no snow yet. I'm thinking of Inuits on the tundra north of Moosejaw, of my sister in Toronto having a session with the past-life regression therapist, of Proust eating madeleines, of old lovers whose last names I can't remember, of my son in San Francisco taking his girl dancing, of a child in prison in South Africa, of an Arctic whale on his way south, of the Cliffs of Dover on a sunny day, of Trotsky in Mexico, of a servant in old England shaking out a dust rag, of the Cloisters above the Hudson, of a rose in my garden blooming even after the last killing frost. Today I'm cooking for old friends and new friends, for friends with whom I have to make amends and for all the memories of the past. Today I'm making a Ghost Supper.

Where the Real World Is

EVERY WEEKDAY MORNING at 10:30, just about the time the last commuter to Traverse City sixteen miles away has passed down M-22 through Suttons Bay, the old men of the village and the small shopkeepers and the farmers from the surrounding countryside begin to wend their way to what may well be the ten thousandth meeting of the Suttons Bay International Coffee Club.

For thirty-seven years the townsmen have been meeting this way, in what might be described as a modern version of the old "cracker-barrel"—men sitting around the general store, talking. "We've met in about every restaurant or bar in Suttons Bay," says B. J. DeBoer, a retired dry cleaner and the only surviving founding member. "We met here at Boone's Prime Time Pub when it used to be Bert Dumas' Bar. It's been a lot of things in between. We've met at restaurants that don't exist in this town any more."

Boone's is a 1970s-style bar with lots of natural wood, hanging ferns, a fireplace, and blow-dried bartenders. It is not exactly what one would imagine as a "cracker-barrel" setting, but the men don't come here to satisfy some quaint image of themselves. They come here for the thing itself. "Three months in the coffee club is worth two years of Harvard," cracks Vic Steimel, an older member of the group who says, when asked his age, "If you're looking for really old ones, I was here when they dug the hole for the bay."

A lot of the men in the club are retired; they come here partly because they have more time to have coffee than younger men and partly because the years have taught them that an essential ingredient of sanity and balance is contact with others who are not like them.

"We spend too much time with people who are just like us," says Ed Marshall, a real estate agent from across the street. "People are afraid to talk with strangers, especially in cities. We're cut off—as a nation—more than we've ever been. TV has taken over communication. Conversation is a lost art." He pauses for a minute, takes a sip of his coffee, and then says, "Small towns don't have a lot of scope, but this is where the real world is. Most people don't realize this."

Embryonic democracy, that's what the International Coffee Club of Suttons Bay represents. It is not the full-fledged democracy of a nation, complete with lofty ideals and political structure. It is the *instinct* for democracy, the yearning in the individual human for awareness of the whole of humankind, of which each individual is an integral part.

Here there are plumbers, carpenters, lawyers, cherry growers, and undertakers. Some of the men are descendants of Suttons Bay's first Norwegian settlers, people who chose this bay within a bay of Lake Michigan because it reminded them of the fjords of Norway. Others, like Ed Marshall, are resorters who have become local residents. Ed sells real estate and his wife, Mally, is the proprietor of the Suttons Bay Bookstore. Mally Marshall's Barnard degree, coupled with her intense love and knowledge of books, makes this bookstore more sophisticated than one might expect for a hinterland town the size of Suttons Bay (population five hundred thirty-nine). "You have to have a very decided philosophy of life to make it up here," Ed Marshall says. "A view of the bay and half the pay and all that."

A statewide issue percolates in the coffee club, but neither boils over nor becomes particularly noticeable. Robert Moody, thirty-three, is a Suttons Bay businessman who wants to offer a "basic" cremation service for six hundred dollars—"or less," he says, "once I build my own crematorium over at Williamsburg." Ray Martinson, the town undertaker, whose family has owned the funeral parlor across the street since the turn of the century, is vehemently opposed, as are most undertakers in the state. But the issue doesn't come up.

"Oh, sometimes Ray will move to the other end of the table," Moody says.

"Be careful what you say to that reporter," Moody's attorney, Jim Williams, warns as he heads out the door to his office across the street (it's eleven o'clock and the group is breaking up). "You might be *accurately* quoted, Moody. That would be your undoing."

Moody confides to me that he wrote his high school term paper on cremation and that "the controversy" has been written up in the *New York Times*.

"We asked Moody to buy pancakes for everyone on Ash Wednesday," B. J. DeBoer says.

Outside, some of the men are standing around on the sidewalk talking. Henry Upjohn, a retired downstate businessman, is talking to Haaken Clausen, a local plumber. Upjohn is wearing a black and white houndstooth-checked hat with marvelously long earflaps—like a dachshund's. The sun is very bright. Upjohn is explaining why oxen can't be taught to back up.

Inside the men are flipping pennies to see who has to pay. "Whoever loses most in a year has to be president," someone says.

"We don't have any rules or regulations. We don't have any membership requirements. We let women in here. We let grandchildren in here. We let Norwegians in here," says Conway Smith, a cherry grower. "The only rule is, 'One is offended if one is not offended.' There are no cliques or factions."

How far the boundaries of this particular swatch of democracy, of Americana, might conceivably be stretched is unclear. Could women really come in here? Could blacks or Indians or Jews come in here? In theory, yes; in practice, it's not known. They don't.

But even the purest ideas are not always pure in practice. The Greeks, who are credited with coining the idea of democracy, kept slaves. It is the idea that counts, we know, for in the long course of human history, each idea can be improved upon. Certainly if there were a million "international coffee clubs," if each small town, each city block, had one, the world would be an immeasurably more pleasant place, with its million small democratic prisms.

Graduation Day at Lake Leelanau St. Mary's

ONE SPRING EVENING when I was a child, my father took me fishing in the small village of Lake Leelanau. The village was at the narrows of the twenty-mile-long lake by the same name. There was an old rickety wooden bridge there, and it was from this that we fished. Overhead was a newer, concrete bridge and I remember the sound the cars made going across it and the way the bridge hummed—tzrromm, tzrromm—long after the cars had gone.

There was also in this village, on the shores of the lake, an ancient Catholic school. I remember the old cobblestone buildings, the broad lawns and the lake, the long shadows of late spring at eight o'clock and people strolling in the golden light.

There are ways in which certain scenes, those observed from a train or car window, or certain magazine illustrations, those mindlessly gazed at while sitting in a doctor's office, impress themselves on one's mind so that they become images in the memory bank indistinguishable from the memories in one's own life, as if one had lived those moments, or is remembering them for some purpose as yet not encountered. And that's the way it was with that cobblestone church on the banks of that lake, as if the image was being saved for later use.

Now I live in the village of Lake Leelanau, for reasons no more complex than those of people the world over who live twenty miles from where they grew up. The church and school are still there, although the Dominican nuns are gone.

The village, which was faded even in the 1950s when I fished there with my father, is further faded now, and on back streets old stores have been converted to apartments with here and there an old barber pole or "Salada Tea" sign marking the way to someone's dwelling. The rerouting of the main highway in the 1940s forever changed this village so that now traffic goes around it instead of through it, and the town seems to exist just at the edge of real life.

Yet some things never change, it seems. In the spring of 1987, its centennial year, I attended graduation ceremonies at Lake Leelanau St. Mary's. One of my neighbors invited me; that was how I found myself walking between cobblestone buildings in long-shadowed golden light, almost as if time had collapsed around three decades, and suddenly I was living in the moment of the image or the memory.

It is May, trout-fishing weather. Thirteen seniors stand on the lawn in front of the school, waiting to go to rehearse commencement speeches and routines over at the church. They are waiting for Principal Mike Knoff and parish priest Father Francis Partridge. The air smells like wet grass.

A hundred robins sing, telling of rain. It is warm. Down near the lake a willow bends to limpid water. A trout jumps. On the hill across the lake, clouds move like smoke across a white orchard, while near at hand the sun breaks through in golden shafts above the dusty playground.

"Let's not graduate," says Cathy Sue Kishevsky. "Let's just go and have a party and come back."

Someone plucks a newly-hatched caddis fly from Cathy's yellow sweater, carefully pulling the sticky legs free of the knitted yellow whorls and letting this aphrodisiacal food of brook trout loose in the humid air.

Dandelion fluffs are blowing; poplar blossoms, fluffy and pale, are blowing across the lawn, across the road, across on the breeze.

Snow melted here a month ago. Now it is spring: spring in the muddy two-track alley, spring on the fence rows, wood piles, and backyard gardens. Pictures in the centennial yearbook show that the village and school haven't changed much in a hundred years. Some of these students' parents met and fell in love here, and some of their grandparents are buried in the cemetery up the hill. All of them at some time watched the branches of the willow sweep the water of the lake, heard the trout jump, and saw the clouds move across the hills on a spring day.

Principal Mike Knoff comes down the steps. We walk across the lawn to the church. The air is dense with moisture, a million tiny dots verging on the brink of rain. Frogs are calling; in the road are several that died trying to make the annual crossing from marsh to lake. As we walk along we pass a lovely old cobblestone building that does not appear to be in use. The building is part of the former convent, English teacher Judy Yoder explains. The building sits empty because the parish cannot afford to renovate it.

In the church narthex are brochures: Focus on the Family; I Am the Way, the Truth, and the Cross; Power in Parenting; The Young Child; Blessed Are the Poor in Spirit; Marriage— What It Could Be; Annual National Honor Society; All You Can Eat Spaghetti Dinner; Pew Renovation Project; The Family under Fire.

In the church, pale light shines through stained glass windows. Novena candles burn. Sister Mary Edward in black habit rearranges chrysanthemums on the altar. Mrs. Yoder asks the seniors if they want to get more flowers, some of the lilacs or apple blossoms that are blooming everywhere. Sister Mary Edward says she believes they have enough flowers. "This is what happens when you graduate; you have to make all these decisions—more flowers, not," Mrs. Yoder says.

Under the stained glass windows are names: Thomas Plamondon, Mrs. John Nolan, Paul Plamondon, Mrs. Emil Grant, and Jacob W. Schaub. I pull out an old bulletin from the rack in the pew in front of me. "Instruct me, O Lord, in the

way of your statutes, that I may observe them" (Psalm 119:33).

"Line up alphabetically," Mrs. Yoder says. She is a woman with a long blonde ponytail, a 1972 graduate of St. Mary's. "After Mr. Knoff says, 'I'm introducing the class of 1987'— that's when you turn and face the audience and move your tassels over to the left."

The principal begins to rehearse the procession of seniors into their respective places, calling out their names: "Esther Ackerman, Michael Leonard Bodus, Deborah Jean Couturier, Joseph Edward Deegan, Cathy Sue Kishevsky, Mary Jo Korson, Scott Allan Linguar, Todd Eugene Morton, Ethel I. Rosales, Peter Mathew Schaub, Chris Elaine Sharnowski, Todd Michael Stallman, Matthew Wade Tarsa." This could be a roll call in a dream.

Michael Bodus, the class valedictorian, is sitting next to me in a church pew. "I enjoy the atmosphere of the school," he says. "The relationship between teachers and students is like a family. We know everybody's life history. People know what you're going to do before you do it. The teachers are aware of you. They take time with you."

"Mr. Bodus, get in your position. This may be a minor point, but it'll really work better if you turn like this [clockwise] when you take your places," Mrs. Yoder says. "Please, people, when you go up and stand, don't talk to the person in front of you or hit him in the back of the knees. Don't come in shorts tonight. Even if you have beautiful legs. Shirts. Shoes. Ties. Simple."

The students, released from the graduation rehearsal, have the rest of the day off. The younger students, seeing the seniors head for their cars and call to each other across the lawn, look wistfully after them as they themselves return to the suddenly dull, chalkboard school, the hot spaghetti lunch in the refectory in the basement of the school. The day seems very dim and lackluster now, as if a light had gone out; in fact the sun seems unable to pierce a dense gray spring sky.

Up the stairs after lunch, past the bulletin board that says, "Let There Be Peace on Earth, and Let It Begin with Me," past the first- and second-grade display of macaroni art, is the fifth- and sixth-grade class—two grades together at the elementary level and all mixed together in the high school. Teacher Molly Petroskey hears reports on George Washington.

"I thought George Washington was the kind of guy who didn't keep slaves," a little boy comments when the report is over.

"He was, but he needed them," the girl giving the report answers.

"Maybe he treated his slaves differently," the teacher offers.

The student giving the report says, "He was kind to his slaves."

Outside the robins are singing; the mist is rising from the lake. The long narrow windows frame the roofs of the town and the hills the way they always did.

The children, released for recess, stream down the stairs, past a bulletin board that says, "My Foot Is on the Path," with pastel construction paper letters and pastel construction paper birds and flowers.

"The day begins with prayers," Mrs. Petroskey says. "That's another way we feel close. If a kid is worried about his parents taking a trip on a plane, we all pray for them; everyone is aware of that child all day, and the kid knows that other people care."

Mrs. Petroskey went to school here as a child, and now after living in Boston for two decades she and her artist husband, Fred Petroskey—who also went to school here as a child—have retired back here. The field behind their house now, Molly says, touches the field that was the far edge of her parents' farm, where she used to play as a child, and now she can look out her kitchen window and see that field and feel the overlapping time frames, the overlapping realities, of her's and others' lives. "It's sort of like you get a second chance to appreciate this," she says. "I say to my kids, 'Look at that steam rising off the lake in the narrows,' because some day you won't see this."

In the old yearbooks are pictures of Molly McGee and Fred Petroskey at the prom, Molly and Fred in the high school play. "It's very odd to come back," Molly says. "It's like going back in time to the early 1930s—without the Depression. I see myself walking up the stairs on the same floors. The bathrooms are painted the same. I'm teaching my friends' grandchildren, and they look just like their grandparents did."

The children come in from recess.

I walk down to the grocery store, down the quiet streets of this village with its old stores no longer in use. The St. Mary's church and school, although still the center of the Catholic community, are not the center of the entire community as they once were. Summer resorters, retirees from cities, newcomers to the community, commuters to Traverse City—they all live their lives, in most cases, as if the church and school did not exist.

N.J.'s grocery story is the main business in the town. It is quiet in the middle of this May afternoon—subdued, in sync with the waiting-for-graduation mood that lies on the village and the school. The floors are newly painted, in preparation for the tourists and summer resorters who will come to this village in a few days, Memorial Day weekend. But not yet.

In the dead air that exists between the afternoon of graduation and the onslaught of the tourist season, in the temporary vacuum, the illusion that the past is present is almost palpable. In the sweet, humid, flower-scented afternoon, the village does seem to hold the ineffable air of an earlier, more neighborly time, a time of sidewalk conversations and backyard kitchen gardens, almost as if the ghosts of these things exist just beyond perception and could be summoned by holographic science or clairvoyance.

I buy a Coke and drink it in The Grove park and read the Traverse City paper before walking home along M-204.

As I walk, the sun disappears behind a cloud. Suddenly it is cold. The wind blows low upon the ground. The gravel and sand hills, the glacier-gouged valley, seem alien and the humans here, temporal: churches, schools, construction paper flowers, suddenly wispy, make-believe.

How the prose of other people's everyday lives can seem like poetry to those, like myself, who have never experienced such ordinariness so un-self-consciously, I am thinking. Yet, as easy as it is to appreciate the guileless innocence of Lake Leelanau St. Mary's, how much harder it is to be a part of it within the context of a more expanded and complex reality.

In order for this village community to come alive and really live again in the old way, new people coming in will have to be able to identify with it, with its values, and have practical reasons for being a part of it; nostalgia alone won't do it, and the chill I feel is partly that realization.

It threatens rain all afternoon, but by 7:30 that evening the sky is first weakly clear and then a mass of brilliant pink and crimson. Red sunset light shines through the stained glass windows and through the open door of the church—where now five priests in long black gowns and long black beards, except for clean-shaven Father Partridge—come in like ancient geese, truckling down the aisle so solemnly.

Then come the graduates, grave and giddy by turns.

From the balcony, a male tenor begins to sing Bette Midler's "The Rose," in a voice of such sweetness and melody that people in the pews down below like myself who have not looked at their programs, turn their heads in sudden surprise to see Kevin Tarsa, and next to him Steven Tarsa, singing for their brother Matt's graduation.

The principal says a prayer, "Almighty God, we gather tonight to honor our graduates. . . ."

The bishop asks, "How does my life reflect my faith? Am I using my time to make this world a better place?"

Vaguely I am contemplating the bishop's vestments, the alpha and omega symbols on the altar cloth, hearing simultaneously the baby crying and the robin singing; these are signatures of the daily and the eternal, the universal and the immediate, in this coming-in and going-out place for this community, this place of baptisms and weddings and funerals and graduations, for the last one hundred years.

Then as quickly as it began, it is over. Kevin Tarsa sings "Eagle's Wings," and we are all swept out into the warm spring air.

The Peace Ribbon

It BEGAN over dinner with friends in the warm, early spring that has now passed. Something about the night—my friends being very much in love, the spars of northern lights through their dining room windows, the gentle way our kids played together and then fell asleep in front of the TV—gave a tender feeling to the entire evening. And it was this evening that I learned about the peace ribbon.

Women from all over the United States, my friend said, were embroidering pieces of a ribbon that would be wrapped around the Pentagon on August 4, 1985, in memory of the bombing of Hiroshima and Nagasaki and in protest of all nuclear war. Already, she said, they had more than ten miles of ribbon at the ribbon center in Denver, and it was going to take a semi truck to haul it all to Washington, D.C. She invites me to join a group of women working on "the ribbon."

That night I fell asleep dreaming of this truck, trailing ribbon, making its way across the Chagallian night landscape of Iowa, past farmhouses sleeping in the violet starlight and cows in back pastures chewing in slow rhythm.

But when I awoke an hour or two into my sleep, it was to the sound of horrible death screams and a nightmare about a Viking raid in an ancient Scotland where my Celtic ancestors, victorious, are lining the harbor with Viking heads on posts to discourage further Viking hoards. It takes a minute for me to realize that the sharp screams are still continuing and that the cat has apparently trapped a rabbit in the woodpile. Sleepily, I roust out, to go release the rabbit and corral the cat and put her in the woodshed.

The night is still warm, and there is a strange, not unpleasant, sound in the air, a high, faint sound like someone playing the radio on Venus or celestial whales calling to each other, or maybe just the limb above my head squeaking in a slightly musical way. I can't tell. In my present state I feel a confusing mixture of disquietude from the nightmare and soothing calm from the unseasonably mild weather.

After making sure the rabbit is safe at the edge of the woods, I sit on the picnic table in the backyard thinking that there is no reverence for life in nature. Drive for life, yes. The cat kills the rabbit. The owl kills the cat. The Russians kill us, or would if we didn't have enough nuclear warheads. I wouldn't be sitting here at this picnic table thinking about this, I am thinking, if hundreds of aboriginal ancestors before me hadn't been willing to kill someone or something in order to live. The instinct for war is in me, too. I prefer confrontation to silent submission. I relish a good fight. What am I doing embroidering a peace ribbon? It occurs to me then that there is such a thing as fighting when life, liberty, or principle is involved, when not fighting would be worse than dying. Where would we be if the Nazis had won? What about the American Civil War or a hundred other righteous wars? It isn't so much that war is morally wrong, but that our weapons have outstripped us. A nuclear war is unwinnable—unless the other side decides not to fight back, which is unlikely.

What the peace ribbon women are proposing, however, is exactly that: not fighting back. Sandy Miller, one of the women I talk to, says she has concluded that life under the Russians can't possibly be worse than no life at all. But what about all the other rage-filled countries that could get the bomb and start a war? What about the PLO or the Iranians or Nicaragua? Well, she says, she couldn't do anything about that. But she could make a statement against nuclear war. She didn't have to condone it by silence.

Time passes. Early crocus spring gives way to buggy near-summer. The Jehovah's Witnesses get me on their calling route. Teresa from Kentucky sits on my living room sofa telling me about Armageddon. "This will not be man's war, but God's war," says Teresa, who once had a guru in Cincinnati and who looks uncannily like Diane Keaton in *Mrs. Soffel*. "We are in the last of the latter days, when evil spirits, which we know are fallen angels, are trying to take over the world." Teresa is accompanied by Dena, a teeny tiny mail-order bride from the Philippines (I picture her arriving in the envelope) who has married a local man many years her senior.

Like Madame Defarge, I embroider while Dena peppers me with heavily accented quotes from the Bible and Teresa tries to cut Dena off and deliver her own rote-like quotes from the Bible. I am fascinated by these women: by their faith, by their aggressiveness, by their prissiness. "What are you working on?" Teresa finally asks me with a forced little smile. This is my moment. "I'm working for world peace," I tell her, "the end of all wars." Perhaps it's the way I say it, or perhaps the absurdity of this itself strikes them, or perhaps it's simply that their proselytizing time is up, but they leave then.

The morning all the ladies for the peace ribbon are supposed to get together, it had rained hard the night before, then cleared slightly, with a fierce wind. By the time I drive through the village of Lake Leelanau at 9:00 A.M. the air is gray and humid and the trees are the sharp, almost neon, chartreuse you get only in the spring after a rain.

Two nuns, their black dresses whipping around them in the wind, are trying to chase a wounded swan back across the bridge and down off the causeway. The white of the swan matches the wimples around the nuns' faces, and the swan's black beak matches their dresses. The proportionate colors and the shooing motions make it all seem oddly choreographed. Meanwhile, a brindled cow stares at me from a vacant field, and an old woman wends her way down the hill by the steepled church, a wicker market basket over her arm. Lake Leelanau

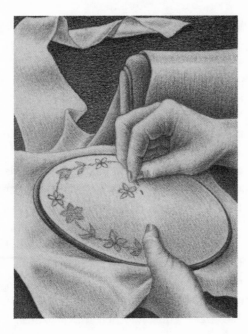

seems to exist not only in its own time warp, but in a time warp that is also a vortex that will suck me down into it.

When I finally cross the bridge it is as if I am driving into the present century. It occurs to me then that the women on the bridge and the woman coming down the hill in Lake Leelanau probably don't think about the eventuality of a nuclear holocaust. It is mostly the people of my generation, people in their late thirties or early forties, who are preoccupied with this. Whether it is because we have more to lose or are more insecure or are more civic-minded isn't at all clear to me.

Bev Cheadle, the woman who has organized our particular group of ladies, has a house high on a hill with a narrow view of Lake Michigan through the trees. She is a woman in her early thirties with a halo of pale, wispy blonde hair and a soft voice. "In the winter," she says, "I had dreams of mushroom clouds, of nuclear holocaust. Working on the ribbon project helped me work through some of that, and do something positive with my energy, and show my children that I'm doing something and so are our neighbors."

As the house begins to fill up with women and children, Laurie Davis, Bev's neighbor and my friend who first told me about the ribbon project, comes over with a pot of fresh coffee. Bev pulls trays of warm apple-bran muffins from the oven, and children flit in and out, grabbing muffins. "To me," Laurie says, noshing on a muffin, "the whole idea of thousands of women all over America creating something beautiful with their own needlework that is also a political statement for peace, a spiritual statement—that's quite a piece of the collective unconscious, if you ask me. And the more people there are who are thinking about peace the stronger the idea gets. It builds positive energy. *Love is stronger than death.*"

"It's a feminist statement," says a hugely pregnant Gerry Simkins. "Men make guns, women make babies. It's time for the women to be heard."

Mavis Bottenhorn, a young mother of a toddler and an infant—in between changing diapers, wiping noses, and kissing "hurts"—is scrambling across the floor, pins in her mouth, trying to pin the pieces of the peace ribbon together. It would be heartless to pursue this young matron to the other side of the patchwork, asking, "But do you think it will really do any good?"

I feel slightly absurd and naive, standing around drinking coffee in this kitchen, a little like someone attending a symposium to ban evil, along with these other very sincere, slightly absurd and naive ladies, most of whom would probably think banning evil was a good idea. But then I think about the other side, the Pentagon with its gold NORAD phone that doesn't work—the one they're supposed to use to communicate on in case of nuclear attack. I think about Reagan's "joke" about bombing the Russians. I think about American presidents generally—Carter prattling on about lascivious thoughts in the interview with *Playboy,* Andrew Jackson who thought the world was flat—and I come to the conclusion that this little group of ladies embroidering for peace is not so absurd by comparison.

It's just that human life, in the face of nuclear threat, takes on a surreal quality. It is then that we realize our duality, how recently we evolved from the muck and acquired—somewhere along the mucky way—a soul. Willy-nilly pursuing our animal instinct for survival, for killing, like the cat with the rabbit, we have—at the same time, bozo-like—created the means for our own annihilation on a hair-trigger. We are at a point in our history where we can now see with breathtaking clarity how experimental the union of matter and spirit has been.

An Afternoon on
Archie's Islands

EVERY LATE SUMMER, my old friend Archie comes by and begins to reminisce about "the islands." Drummond, North Manitou, South Manitou, South Fox—he lived on these islands, on and off, for years. Now approaching seventy, he talks about leaving the Leelanau Peninsula and going back. He says he would have old George Grosvenor, the boatman, drop him off. He says he'd take enough food for the winter, some books, and he'd take an old dog.

I can picture the kind of day it always is when he comes by to talk about the islands. It is late summer, dead still. Jays are calling, and there is a dull, grayish cast to the underside of leaves. It is canning season.

It is that kind of day now, and Archie and I are sitting at the picnic table in my backyard drinking iced tea out of wide-mouthed mason jars. My three-year-old stands on her swing and sings "Old MacDonald" at the top of her voice. She is at that age where her behavior teeters between the cute and the excessively cute. We are a trio: an old man, a middle-aged woman, and a three-year-old.

Archie and I are both companied-out and summered-out. It is a good day to think about islands. "You can feel it the minute you step off the boat; you're away from things," he says and pauses a minute, staring into his tea. "I just like to be there when the mist rolls in, which it usually does."

It is rare that a person has lived on any one of the less populated northern Lake Michigan islands for any length of time; Archie is in a class alone in that he has lived on several. He started living on North Manitou when he was eighteen. "That was when they had the farm there. Had cattle. Had orchards. Had a crew of eight or nine men." Later, most of North Manitou was purchased by a foundation and converted to a private deer preserve. Archie worked there, too. "They had executives from International Harvester out of Chicago, Century Boat, Detroit Diesel, Cesna Group. Arthur Godfrey used to come with the boys from Continental Motors." It staggers the imagination to try to picture talent-show host Arthur Godfrey on North Manitou. I asked Archie what Arthur Godfrey was like. "He liked to be the center of the floor all the time," Archie recalls. "We realized that. Surely he wasn't going to be any different on the island."

Later, Archie worked cutting timber on South Manitou. By this time he was raising four kids alone. "I frankly enjoyed it," he says. "I had the kids, their cousins. Whoever came. We stayed in one of those abandoned houses over there. Had everything. Had utensils in the kitchen. Had an organ in the living room. Kids slept upstairs. First night, they said there were spooks. So they wanted to sleep outside. I said, 'OK, you got your choice: mosquitoes or spooks.' They must have preferred the spooks. They moved back inside."

The kids had rotten-egg fights at Gull Point, swam in South Manitou Bay, met the boat on "boat day," and ate canned chicken off the shipwrecked *Francisco Morazan*. It was a Huck Finn life. One night Archie took them up to sleep in the Valley of the Giants—an area in the South Manitou dunes where huge dead trees stand careening in the sand. "The moon was full. The trees made weird shadows. I said, 'Kids you gotta see this.' I had an old beat-up pickup truck I drove. I took 'em all out there with their blankets and sleeping bags. We spent the night up there." He pauses a minute. "I don't think they let you out in those dunes anymore." He pauses again. "South Manitou's completely changed since they got the [Sleeping Bear Dunes] National Park in there. Last time I was over there they had this little ranger following me around with a beeper. What the hell was he following me around for?" Archie laughs, "I wasn't gonna steal a *bush*."

As far as Archie is concerned, the national park rangers on the island are completely contrary to the idea of islands. "An islander's a different breed of cat," Archie says, getting that slow smile as he remembers something. "I remember a carpenter on Drummond Island—we called him 'Boone's Farm' because that's all he ever drank. Guess he got drunk on it, too. Guess you could if you drank three or four bottles. Only went to the mainland once a year to register for unemployment.

"Friend Hank had a beer joint on Drummond, went back to Detroit for a funeral. Grew up in Detroit. Got over in the wrong lane, I guess. Cops ticketed him. He came back to the island, madder'n hell, said he was never going to leave the island again. I don't think he did, either."

Drummond Island, Archie says, really should be part of Canada, not Michigan. "At least that's the story they tell on Drummond," he says. "How a team of American and English surveyors came down the St. Mary's River along toward dark, and how the Americans got the Englishmen drunk and took them down around the east side of the island in the night. Americans wanted the island real bad because of the dolomite."

Now Archie thinks that if he went back to the islands, he would go back to South Fox, a small island off the Lake Michigan shore at Charlevoix. "There's nothing out there. What the hell do you need, anyway? Seems like you always have what you need on the island. You don't crave anything. Seems like on the mainland, there's always something you want. Gotta get in your car. Gotta go get something all the time. I'd be at peace out there. I wouldn't know what was happening on the mainland. I'd be just as happy not to know."

When Archie leaves I put my small daughter down for a nap. I feel oddly restored. Vicariously, I've been off the mainland all afternoon.

Mozart and Ace on
Omena Bay

THE HARBOR BAR at Omena sits in a tuck of the bay, at a place where the bay curves in and the highway curves out, so that the two almost touch, except that in between is the Omena Harbor Bar. Its patrons have usually included a few Omena regulars and people from the nearby Indian community. It's a plain kind of bar with a rickety wraparound porch and a good view of the water. Old gas pumps, now out of use, are on the highway side, and on the other side boats are docked so close to the bar they almost seem tethered there.

The bar is one of about five commercial buildings in Omena, the others being a country store, an ancient U.S. Post Office, a grocery store converted to an art gallery, and the fire station. There are about a dozen villages like Omena, give or take a few buildings, scattered over the Leelanau Peninsula, a county of rolling hills, cherry orchards, dunes, and ninety miles of Lake Michigan shoreline—with an indigenous Indian population, several generations of Polish, French, and Norwegian immigrants, about twenty years' worth of hippies, and several thousand summer tourists. Except for the tourists, we are an isolated, unsophisticated population. We do not as a rule have live music in our bars or ever see black people.

In the beginning some people say they heard the music floating out over the water from the Omena Harbor Bar. Others say they heard it when they were walking by on the road. After that it was word of mouth in a county with only fifteen thousand people, most of whom were either related or friends or people who knew each other from work or church.

By late July, farmers, bricklayers, wealthy lawyers, poor artists, librarians, and summer visitors were all flocking to the Omena Harbor Bar to experience what had become a Leelanau County cultural event. By August some local people had taken out an ad in the *Leelanau Enterprise* "to thank John 'Ace' Davis and Mozart Perry for the fine entertainment and wonderful summer." By September the owner of the Omena Harbor Bar was running "held over" ads in the *Enterprise*.

It was a warm Sunday in early September before my husband and I and our two daughters got up to the Omena Harbor Bar to hear the people who, by this time, were simply called "the musicians." We'd heard Sunday was the day they played from 4:00 to midnight with an open mike. Other families like ours were already there when we arrived, giving the place an oddly innocent, after-church air.

Davis is a tall man with a wide smile who stands with his arm around his bass and talks to the audience as if we were all at a family reunion. Perry is shorter, quieter, and sits at his electric piano, looking down through his glasses like an owl, with a look on his face of someone about to smile. Davis announces to the audience that they have seven books of songs with a thousand songs each, dating back to 1895 and up through the 1940s. He invites requests. They begin playing Cole Porter's "Night and Day."

It is pressure-cooker muggy in the room, pickle-canning weather. The bay is clouding over and it feels like it might rain. Davis takes a request on a cocktail napkin and turns to Perry, "Mozart, what can we do for Chubs on his birthday?" He could be talking about his cousin.

"We'll think of somethin'," Perry says, and in a moment he has launched into a surprisingly wild and joyful version of "When the Saints Come Marchin' In," his fingers a blur over the keyboard, his eyes a ruminant, half-closed.

At six they take a break. Under the wisteria vine over the steps of the Tamarack Craftsmen Gallery across the road, Perry says he grew up in Toledo in the 1920s when it was a little like Leelanau County. "There was no dope. You could leave your screen door unlocked and sleep on your back porch. All people had was church and the picture show. That's what made good musicians. People took patience with their music."

Perry says he got his name from an aunt who "played a little piano," and that he was influenced by Art Tatum, another Toledo jazz pianist. Both Davis and Perry say they are primarily self-taught and were in their late forties before they became full-time musicians. They've been working together nineteen years. "We don't drink, we don't smoke, and we eat right," Davis says. "We want to be able to get out of bed and get back to work the next morning. Mozart and I, we're on the band-stand for the *art* of music, for the *joy* of it. The joy of music is built on love, love of life, your fellow man."

Back across the street they open with a cool, light version of "Take the A-Train," and then go into a rousing version of "Route 66," just as heat lightning is ripping over the bay, their playing seemingly synchronized with the rhythms of the weather. A Lake Leelanau mason, LaVern "Zip" Flees, is waiting with his concertina to sit in with them—"Zip the Zipper, the Concertina Man," Ace introduces him. Another man is practicing his trumpet in the parking lot, waiting to come on. Some members of a local dance group have come up from Traverse City "just to dance to music you never hear anymore," Darcy Cunningham says. An Indian man is dancing by himself. Ace says, "Wonderful music. Wonderful people, people enjoying themselves." I recognize a retired banker and his wife and say hello. I overhear someone behind me say, "If I ever have to go to Mars, I want to go with those two guys."

Not everyone appreciates it, however. "I like music with a message," says a disgruntled woodcutter at the bar. "The music of the '60s had a message. Bob Dylan." A woman sitting next to him, a musician herself, says, "They miss notes. They aren't as perfect as everyone says they are."

But Rick Shimel, manager for the Detroit-based rock band, the Buzz Tones, says, "I like to see the life musicians bring to their music and those two cats bring a lot. They come and plug in on a Sunday afternoon and play for eight hours and that's unheard of in this business. They do it because they love it and the audience knows it. There's a hundred years of rich musical history behind them and the audience feels that. Those guys are packing a bar that never had anybody in it and that's a valid act."

Perry and Davis stayed through the fall. They played at the Harbor Bar on weekends and during the week they sometimes played for free for schools and local civic groups.

One day in the winter I called a friend in Boston, Berrien Thorn. Berrien had come to Leelanau County the summer before and had walked into this little bar in Omena and heard Ace and Mozart. He asked them if they knew a song his father had written, "I Hear a Rhapsody." They knew it and played it. Berrien and I talked about music and perfection. "Basho," Berrien says, "the Japanese haiku master, sometimes wrote haiku with either more or less than the perfect number of syllables. When asked about it, Basho said, 'It's not the syllables of the haiku that's important, but the syllables of the heart.' People who complain about their notes have little hearts. Besides, some nights I'm sure they are perfect." Then he talks about a student of Basho's who came to Basho and said, "Master, if you take the wings off a dragonfly, it looks like a saltshaker. That's a great haiku, right?" And Basho says, "No, no, you idiot. You put wings on a saltshaker so it looks like a dragonfly; that's a great haiku."

It is now early spring on the Leelanau Peninsula. The leaves on the trees are the size of mouse ears and the morel mushrooms are coming up in the woods. People are talking about "Mozart and Ace" coming back again this year. Word is that they'll be back at the Harbor Bar by the middle of June; local people are polishing up their instruments and getting out their dancing shoes in preparation.

For my part I can't get that haiku out of my mind. I keep

seeing Leelanau County as a saltshaker with wings on it. And I keep seeing Mozart and Ace—weightless silhouettes floating over Omena Bay with their instruments—light-filled holograms.

The Herbalist's Garden

CONSIDER THIS: The spine of the comfrey leaf has been used for untold ages to sew up wounds and speed healing. Scientists now know comfrey contains allantoin, a bone-knitting and cell-proliferating substance. What challenges the mind confronted with this has nothing to do with what comfrey does or what scientists now know, but rather how anyone ever thought to use the spine of the comfrey plant to sew up a wound in the first place.

A knowledge of plants and a flash of insight like the kind that brought Einstein to his theory of relativity must have led someone, sometime, to this peculiar but effective use of comfrey, and there's a little bit of magic in all that. It's a magic that's missing from our trips to the pharmacist, for instance, where we give the man our money and get a vial of pills and that's it. It must have been more interesting to be sick when we had to go visit the old lady who lived under the hill, and we got a queer-smelling poultice in exchange for a chicken or something.

You think about this and you think about food, too, and the genius and wizardry that goes into that; how dull it would be, for example, if instead of tomatoes with Parmesan, you had three gray capsules. Or you think about some of the unaccountably delectable foods, like eels with green sauce, and you wonder how anyone thought it up and how different life would be if food were replaced with prescriptions with Latinate names.

[53]

So, thinking about this, and wondering about comfrey and Einstein and *anguille au vert,* I found myself one day wending my way out Lime Lake Road and over Overby and across Narlock and down Stachnik to Pan's Forest Herb Garden at Medicine Wheel Center, otherwise known as Lori Cruden's house. There, I knew, in a world of amulets, soul-work healing workshops, fairy flower notecards, and herbs planted in the correct phase of the moon and now flourishing, I would find a little of the magic in life the IRS, throughway cloverleafs, and nine-digit zip codes had taken out of it.

Lori Cruden's herb garden is about twenty feet across, star-shaped, outlined in stone, with three concentric rings of stone around it. Lori, called "Lorien" in her catalog, is standing in the middle of her garden weeding lemon balm.

She is about six feet tall with long red hair and an ethereal quality, like the ladies you see taming unicorns in thirteenth-century monastery tapestries. She is fairly young, thirty-three, but with an old-lady, farmer voice. She's adamantly reclusive and likes her privacy. In spite of inhabiting the normal roles of wife and mother, in spite of having grown up in U.S. suburbia, in spite of being the daughter of a high school English teacher and an American businessman, and in spite of having attended American public schools half her life, she has the air of being from another time and place, a quality of being totally eccentric without half trying. "I wouldn't have lasted in Salem," she says with a throaty laugh.

"The soil is sandy here," she says, toeing it with a size ten tennis shoe. She says she grows her herbs without commercial pesticides, using garlic or cayenne to remove some pests, and uses only organic fertilizers. "I've added goat manure, kitchen compost, leaves. But most herbs like a poor soil, so it's fine for that."

She began her business five years ago with three hundred dollars as capital, took a three hundred dollar loss the first year, and has been making a modest income ever since. "There's big money in herbs now," she says, "not in the kind of business I have but in some of the ones you see on television. It's part of that whole Yuppie self-care thing. Whatever Yuppies like makes money. In some ways that's helped my business. In other ways it's created difficulties. The Food and Drug Administration wants to withdraw some herbs from the market. They're alert to quackery, some of these big companies that want to sell chickweed for thirty dollars a bottle for quick weight loss. Chickweed is a very cheap herb, two dollars a pound. The people I deal with are pretty knowledgeable about herbs. They want to know who grew it, what phase of the moon it was planted in. I have a personal relationship with the herbs and the people I sell them to. I get letters from customers wanting me to stay with them if I'm ever in their area. I got a letter the other day from an Egyptian lady staying in Jamaica, New York, telling me about her pregnancy. I got a letter a while ago from a man raising his son alone. He wanted to know if the amulets I make were too strong for a child's sensitive spirit. So I made him one I thought would be appropriate for his son. The amulets come in little hand-dyed, hand-sewn velvet bags, made for me by a woman in Virginia. A lot of meditative attention goes into each amulet."

Until lately, a knowledge of herbs was widespread. In Shakespeare's day, a half-crazed, suicidal Ophelia could rant about wormwood in *Hamlet,* and everyone knew what she meant. As recently as World War I, sphagnum moss was gathered from swamps and used by the U.S. Army to pack wounds because of its sterility. There's a sense of personal empowerment that comes from the knowledge of herbs, a feeling of connectedness that comes from being able to reach down and pluck something from the ground to cure a headache or treat poison ivy. It's a connectedness that's a kind of amulet in itself in these troubled times—when the nuclear threat and the breakup of AT & T, just to mention a couple of troublesome things, leave everyone feeling a little unconnected. This is only theory, of course.

The question is, how did a girl with an all-American suburban upbringing end up in Pan's Forest Herb Garden meditating over amulets? We have moved inside her no-plumbing, self-built home that smells sweetly of herbs. Lorien folds herself into a chair. She says she was always drawn to stones and plants, the basic elements of the earth; that's where she finds her solace. Then, too, her father was an inspired gardener. When she was a small child, her father invented a way to grow chrysanthemums at night under strings of lights. "It was down in Florida," she says. "I was real little, so to see all these lit-up fields of chrysanthemums at night was magic, like Christmas." Her father lost money on the project, she says, but sold the idea to a company that made millions.

She serves me Cafix, a coffee substitute, in a bowl-shaped red cup. I ask her what's in it, and she reads me the can in a scratchy, matter-of-fact voice: "Roasted malt, chicory, barley, shredded beet roots, and figs." She tells me about the elves in her garden in the same scratchy, matter-of-fact voice. "They aren't like in books," she says, "dressed in little brown suits or anything, although I did have one once who always dressed in a little brown suit. They're more free-form. Some are place oriented and some are plant oriented. Some of the plant-oriented ones came with me when I moved. In the place I lived before, which was older and more forested, the elves were more defined but shyer. Here they're vague energy forms, but brighter, more forthcoming, more curious." She says she has an intuitive approach to gardening and has to be open to energy forms and changes. Some people might find this approach to gardening unusual, but I view benevolent eccentrics—whether gardeners or physicists—as a world resource. They might come upon something the rest of us need to survive.

Anyway, if whales can beach themselves en masse because of mysterious changes in ocean ions, and if certain trees can emit a noxious substance in response to leaf-eating insects, and if scientists can now pinpoint the mood-altering characteristics of sunlight, then I guess someone can find "forthcoming" energy forms in their herb garden. Indeed, this ability might be desirable in an herbalist. For my part, I have never seen an energy form, wearing a brown suit or otherwise, but I would

like to believe they exist, as a counterbalance to mundanity if
nothing else.

When the Mists Part

Waiting for the Millennium

IT'S HARD to remember now how news of the Harmonic Convergence reached me on the Leelanau Peninsula. People were talking about August 16, 1987, as the day everyone was going to help usher in not only a new year, but a new age, one characterized by peace.

Theories about the end of the world as we know it and the beginning of a new one have been around since the Plague. Our country was founded in part by members of millennial sects who thought America was "the New World." But this time, people I knew were talking about it.

A man I knew with a degree from Harvard Divinity School said he was going to observe the Harmonic Convergence. A friend whose daughter was studying to be an Episcopal priest at Yale said her daughter and her daughter's friends in Boston were going to celebrate it. And a social worker friend from Denver called to say that Boulder was a center for organizing the event "globally."

I wanted to see if people who lived around me would go stand on beaches and hilltops at dawn on August 16, so that night I set my alarm clock for 5:00 A.M. When the alarm went off it was dark outside, darker than it should have been at this hour on a summer morning. Was this the millennium? No, it was just overcast. A damp coolness permeated the half-light in my bedroom; outside under the centuries-old maple trees there were pooled dark green lozenges of night.

To get up at dawn in an empty house on an overcast summer morning is to be a child again sneaking through the house at Christmas waiting to find Santa Claus or some startling magic—an angel, an elf, Jesus—speaking to you alone. No one spoke, but still I was waiting.

In my old, dark sagging farmhouse with its lace curtains limp in the humid dawn, my coffee sat steaming in its fat yellow cup on the dining room table. It would rain today.

Surely no one but me would be naive enough to get up at this hour and go stand around somewhere and harmonically converge. The mother of one of my daughter's friends kept calling it the Hormonic Convergence. Even that, I thought, would be unlikely in this muggy, insect-breeding weather.

As I nosed my car through the mist along the shore, it began to rain heavily. I imagined I was on a fool's errand, that this whole thing was a hoax, and I would find—like the time my older sisters told me soap was ice cream—that I was the butt of a joke.

To my amazement, Graham Greene Park near Omena was filled with people—most of them getting drenched, to be sure, but there, nonetheless. There were old people, young people, and, judging from the cars, rich people and poor people. Some of them looked like they were on their way to church.

The Leelanau Peninsula was a "power point," someone had explained to me earlier in the week, and that's why hundreds of people were going to observe the Harmonic Convergence here. Just like the Great Pyramids at Gisa, someone said, just like Machu Picchu, the Leelanau Peninsula was "a center for spiritual energy." I grew up here, and as a kid I couldn't remember anyone saying this was a power point. I could remember the tourists in the summer saying, "What do you *do* here in the winter?"

Three women I didn't know, but who I thought could tell me what was happening, accepted my invitation to come back with me to my house and dry off. I thought surely someone, probably everyone, would know more about the Harmonic Convergence than I did and would be able to explain it to me,

but people didn't seem to have much of a grasp of it, other than that it was happening "globally."

The rain fell like beaded curtains outside my living room windows. The rain seemed to intensify the green of the trees; even the air seemed green. I made some tea and cinnamon toast, and we sat around and talked. Penny was a therapist from Santa Barbara; Joyce was a teacher from nearby Old Mission, and Jane was a nurse from Traverse City.

"Nature is going to start giving us stuff like this rain," Joyce said. We talked about acid rain, weather patterns, and dying dolphins.

"I have a friend who channels dolphins," Penny said; she stood up and gave us a wonderfully funny, impromptu imitation of her friend's mediumistic "reading" of a dolphin, her body rippling into fish form.

"The dolphins are trying to tell us something," Jane said. "Something's going to happen. We're all getting sick from this pollution."

The conversation wafted, going here and there. It reminded me of other conversations on other rainy days—the kinds of conversations you have when you're on vacation and it rains all week and you stay inside the cottage and play Parcheesi and eat too much.

I simply didn't understand the Harmonic Convergence. People were looking for something, but what? My friends in Denver sent me a published, ten-thousand-word interview with the man who originated the Harmonic Convergence, Jose Arguelles. His talk about "planetary nowness" and "wave harmonics" left me feeling the way I had that rainy Sunday forenoon with those women—as if I were trying to swim up from a deep, green sleep.

A while ago, the *New York Times Magazine* ran an article on the return to religion among intellectuals and their renewed fascination with "the sacred." More recently, the same publication had an article on string-theory physics that mentioned, more casually than it might have ten years ago, the origins of some math in magic. I would say if there is indeed a trend among intellectuals to return to religion, and a willingness among some physicists to consider how physics and mysticism converge, then my friends are part of those trends.

Several of my intellectual friends, although not all of them, were aware of and interested in the Harmonic Convergence. I would have suspected that my friends were an unrepresentative segment of the population, but a woman I know whose daughter is married to a doctor in Salt Lake City said *her* daughter sent her the Arguelles interview. And there were others I knew, too, from all kinds of backgrounds, who celebrated the Harmonic Convergence. *Time* and *Newsweek* reported the event. Some Wall Street brokers—even *before* the crash—went out and stood on beaches and held hands for peace.

I was so curious about the Harmonic Convergence as a national phenomenon—indicative of the national mood, if nothing else—that I kept asking people about it. I must admit I even arranged a brunch just to get people to talk about it.

I got out the Arguelles interview and started quoting from it.

I read a passage in which Arguelles said he arrived at the dates August 16 and 17, 1987—the days that would usher in the twenty-five-year period of transition leading up to the age of peace, which would begin in 2012—by researching the prophecies of Quetzalcoatl. Quetzalcoatl, I announced somewhat challengingly, was a mythic winged serpent.

But this didn't particularly bother anyone. "How do we know Jesus was really the son of God?" someone countered. "What about the Virgin Birth?"

My friend Stephanie said the Harmonic Convergence could be seen as "a poetic concretization of the Zeitgeist," and added that it was a kind of "shine, Tinkerbell, shine" exercise for peace.

My husband said millennial movements, although they might not be based in reality as we know it, can mobilize people and give them the energy and inspiration to make the transition to a new phase of development.

Since the Harmonic Convergence back in August, summer has come and passed; the stock market has crashed—as predicted not only by new-age psychics, but by reputable economists—and the mood of the country seems to be that of waiting for the other shoe to drop. In keeping with this mood, I've been reading historian Barbara Tuchman's *A Distant Mirror,* a book about the Dark Ages, and I am continually struck by the similarities between those times and our own.

There was a passage about the Plague in one of my old high school history books; in one scene people from a small village in France stand on a hill at dawn and sing and dance and hold hands because they've been told by their parish priest that the Black Death will not strike communities of happy people. The pathetic helplessness of those people, their whistling in the dark, struck me then and strikes me doubly now because now I can identify with it.

Somewhere I've heard that the children's nursery rhyme "Ring around the Rosie" is a song from the Plague years; maybe "ring around the rosie" is what the villagers sang, and "ashes, ashes, we all fall down" is what happened in spite of the singing.

These gloomy thoughts, my own personal plague, are the mood our northern November engenders—when summer is gone, and the tourists and the songbirds are gone, too.

Every day now, the earth turns further from the sun. Our landscape itself seems turned inward, introspective, and the sun is a pale, Van Gogh swirl that appears at noon and then vanishes.

In this starkest of seasons, it is a little hard for me to recall that I went and stood on the beach last summer—along with about five hundred other people—at 5:00 A.M. in a pouring rain and hoped that some good would come of it. I don't know that I prayed for peace—although I probably should have—because I was just too stunned to find myself standing there.

I think I was on that beach during the Harmonic Convergence, in retrospect, and maybe some of the other people were too, because we live in a world with problems so terrible, they are beyond a normal person's control or even comprehension. What to do about holes in the ozone? Potential nuclear holocaust? AIDS? The abuse and neglect of children?

"Chaos demands to be recognized and experienced," Herman Hesse said, "before letting itself be converted to a new order." I hope that's the stage we're in now. I hope our little rain-soaked band on the beach last summer was the first step toward recognizing the chaos—as opposed to being another manifestation of it. I also hope the next step will be to convert the chaos to a new order.

Art's Artists

DAVID GRATH is an artist and a friend of mine who lives in Leland, and I often run into him around town. One day in the Leland Library he mentioned that he was going down to Art's Bar in Glen Arbor that night for the weekly artists' potluck. I'd been hearing about this group for a year or two from friends of mine who were in it, and so that night I decided to join them to see what it was like to get together with a bunch of Leelanau County artists for an evening.

The Leelanau Peninsula has for years been a draw to artists and writers, and this group was the natural result of what happens when enough people of like mind and temperament come together in one place. The county has several other groups like it, in style if not in substance, ranging from dancers and thespians to environmentalists and intellectuals, even a LaLeche League. I'd been to some of these groups but could never seem to get in the groove; they all seemed to require meetings and memberships and certain activities, even if it was only breastfeeding.

However, the group that met at Art's Bar, I'd been told, just got together to eat and talk. I thought I could handle both the eating and talking activities, and they said I didn't have to be a member, or even an artist, to attend.

And I wanted to see Art's again. I hadn't been in Art's since I'd attended Glen Arbor town-hall dances as a teenager. My girlfriends and I used to go into Art's during the band's intermissions to get a Vernor's or a bag of New Era potato chips, feeling slightly risqué as we entered what we'd been taught to think of as "a den of iniquity."

Years later, perhaps trying to capture something of the same mood, I'd taken a college beau in there over Christmas vacation. In our down coats we sat and had a beer and watched in silent amazement as the white-haired lady tending bar took a Chapstick from the cardboard display rack, used it absentmindedly, and put it back.

The Leelanau Peninsula is not what it was, I find myself thinking as I drive down to Glen Arbor along the winding shore road. I am recalling how in seventh grade Sara Barclay and I used to walk between her house in Glen Arbor and my house a mile out, the sky above us a path of light through the trees. We would talk—considering ourselves as we did to be intellectuals—about poetry and art, knowing little about either but wanting to, and lamenting how boring it was to live in Glen Arbor, never envisioning our peninsula as a future artists' colony.

By the time I arrive at Art's Bar it is almost dark. Inside I learn that Art Sheridan, the original owner, has died and that the bar has been sold to a young couple from Empire. The new owners have added some windows and an excellent kitchen but have had the wisdom not to change the name or add California decor.

At four or five tables pushed together, the same metal-legged tables I had remembered, sit the people who must be the artists. I recognize David Grath and my friend Mary Sutherland. There are fifteen or so more people there, some of whom look familiar. A woman I don't know, but who tells me I'd once attended a party for her daughter Cherie when I was eight, comes over and introduces herself as Ananda Bricker and gives me some brochures on the artists.

"In the United States," one brochure begins, "there are numerous areas which, for often inexplicable reasons, exert an attractive force on creative people, drawing them to locate in close proximity yet remaining independent of one another. Northern Michigan is such a region."

"Write about us, but don't tell where it is, just say we're out there in the mists of northern Michigan somewhere, the mists of Avalon," someone says, jokingly referring to the mythical Isle of Avalon off the coast of England—a place of apple orchards, endless summer, and a chosen few.

"What do you call the kind of chairs we're sitting on?" I ask the man sitting next to me. "Kitchen chairs," he says. He is Bill Allen, a metal sculptor who makes ten-foot-tall ostriches and three-hundred-fifty-pound alligators. The recent recipient of a Michigan Arts Council grant, he says he used the money, in part, to buy the copious amounts of copper wire he uses to shape his animals.

"His animals *look* at you," says Susan Stupka Wilson, a painter and art teacher seated next to him. Bill Allen offers an explanation of why he, and maybe some of the others, finds the Leelanau Peninsula attractive. "I grew up in Indiana," he says. "We summered in southern Michigan near St. Joe. Now a lot of nature down there has been destroyed. The Cook nuclear plant is two miles from where we had our cottage."

Mary Sutherland is seated across from me; the woman next to her looks strikingly like Mary and is in fact her twin. "Trish has just moved in with me," Mary says in her Gilda Radner voice. "It's the dream of a lifetime. I'm not an artist, but they let me come."

"She's our therapist," the woman down the row from her says. "We have to have her here." The woman speaking is Judith McClellan, a single mother who supports herself and her three children with her stained glass art.

"We all work alone," Ananda Bricker says, "so this is to keep us from having cabin fever through the long winters. In the summers we meet on the beach." The group has been meeting faithfully every Tuesday for three years, Ananda says. "How can I possibly tell you what it really is?" she asks. "It's really more special than it appears. There's camaraderie and friendship and work. We've helped each other through deaths, divorces, marriages, loaned each other money—all those normal things that people deal with. We aren't organized. We aren't competitive with each other. That's why it works."

In ancient times the caveman's campfire might have been the place for people to gather in the evening, a place to share stories about how the day had gone, how life was treating one. Art's has replaced the campfire—at least in the little village of Glen Arbor, and the young couple who run it have had the intuitive wisdom to know it; they offer these artists their three-dollar-and-fifty-cent potluck supper of soup, salad, coffee, and roll—and a table to sit at for as long as they like.

We had a group for a while, up at our end of the county, of mostly young, mostly college-educated people, some of us writers. We met every other Thursday night for a potluck supper. But some of us found it hard to meet then, having other commitments, and others of us found it hard to always make a dish to pass. For my part I was discomfited by the homogeneity of the group and would bring, from time to time, uneducated people, people with dyed red hair, psychics, born-again Christians, alcoholics, political conservatives, and streams of children, my daughter's friends.

The group didn't last, making me realize, as I sat there that night in Art's Bar with the Glen Arbor artists, that it is not an easy thing to have a group—of any kind—and make it last. It takes a certain amount of homogeneity, of insularity, so people can feel safe in the group. It takes someone to provide the potluck, something as simple as that, so people don't feel they have to cook in order to get together.

"Usually you'd think a group like this would just flow away and not meet that often," says Bill Allen, who adds that the group means a lot to him because he lives and works alone. "Maybe they've continued to meet because the winters up here are so desolate. There's a common bond, despite differences. I love them all dearly. They're all my good friends."

I liked and admired the people I met in Art's Bar that night and envied their ability to reach out to each other, to not try to figure out who among them were the best artists, as I shamefacedly admit I caught myself doing several times that night. Good, better, best is a lesson we all learn too early and too well in this world, forgetting some other more important lessons about simply being human and enjoying life and each others' company. Or as someone said recently, "The art of living is to live one's life as if it were a work of art." I think the artists in Glen Arbor do that rather well.

Jim Harrison

JIM HARRISON strolls from his Leelanau County farmhouse
into the heat of a drought-plagued day, rubbing his one bad eye
against the light. The eye is blind, but sensitive to light, he
explains. It is May 27, 1988, and Harrison has just returned
from a national book tour that he describes cheerfully as "idi-
ocy, the cult of personality and gossip," adding, "I'm incredibly
bad at it; I'm basically no good at anything except writing."

Jim Harrison, called simply "Harrison" by many people in
Leelanau County, is one of Michigan's foremost poets and nov-
elists and his eighth and newest novel, *Dalva*, has been hailed
by the critics as his best book yet. The *New York Times* reviewer
Michiko Kakatani has called it "an epic portrait of America in a
woman's quest," and writer Louise Erdrich, reviewing *Dalva*
for the *Chicago Tribune*, described the book as "generous,
bighearted, romantic . . . a lovely cat's cradle of a novel."

Earlier novels by Harrison include *Wolf*, *A Good Day to Die*,
Farmer, *Legends of the Fall*, *Warlock*, and *Sun Dog*. He began his
career as a poet in 1965 with *Plain Song*, followed by *Locations*,
Outlyer, *Letters to Yesenin*, *Returning to Earth*, *Selected and New
Poems*, and *The Theory and Practice of Rivers*. Both his first
book, *Plain Song*, and his last, *Dalva*, are dedicated to his wife,
Linda.

The Harrisons have two daughters, Jamie, recently married
and now living in Montana, and Anna, a senior in high school.
The couple has lived in this farmhouse on the Leelanau Penin-

sula for nearly twenty-five years. Once they kept horses here, and neighbors would occasionally see Jamie or Linda out riding, but now they just have the dogs, an Airedale and a setter.

Walking through waist-high grass, so hot it smells like toast, Harrison addresses *Dalva*'s underlying moral theme, saying, "This nation has a history, but it also has a soul history and that's what I was interested in. Our original sin in this country was desecration of the Indians, followed by the importation of slaves. Underlying this is greed. But if you think a BMW is what works for you, just go look at LA. Those people are living and dying in a shit monsoon. Because without moral vision there is no future. Without vision, you die."

Harrison speaks in a voice that sounds like Marlon Brando's in *The Godfather,* a hoarse monotone, as if his vocal cords have been scarred. He is fifty years old, swarthy and stocky. His left eye is blind from a childhood accident. He looks rougher than he is and was once mistaken for Jack Nicholson's bodyguard, something that amused both of them.

I met Harrison once fifteen years ago at a party on the Leelanau Peninsula, when the occasion was the annual New Year's party of neighbor and attorney Dean Robb. Harrison walked up to a buxom young woman and told her she should have her tits cut off; he couldn't have known the woman was recovering from a near-fatal car accident and coma and this was her first week out of the hospital. Later someone explained to the young woman that Harrison was probably drunk or high at the time, or both. On the other hand, I have also seen Harrison come to the rescue of people suffering from the kind of mental anguish that usually means lifelong incarceration in an insane asylum. I have seen him go in like Dr. Christiaan Barnard doing a heart transplant and deftly restore with words alone what others attempt to fix with electric shock treatments.

We arrive at the granary studio, out behind the barn, up the porch steps, into the granary that is still morning cool and smells of new wood. Chief Joseph stares down at us from one wall, out of a faded poster. Harrison says he once taped a dead wasp to the back of Chief Joseph's picture to give it hidden

meaning. The poster is captioned, "Today is a good day to die."
On the opposite wall is a girlie calendar that Harrison explains
in some detail is turned to the wrong month because he considered the November girl's naked buttocks inspiring.

The granary, the place of work and writing, is a kind of
sanctuary, or at least that is the impression. There are many
items of Indian aspect. There's a heron wing, a coyote jawbone,
and a blue feather that Harrison says is a kiva trading feather
from the Pueblo people. There's a small pink pig given to him
by his daughter Anna when she was a little girl, and something
that looks like a dried heart, which Harrison says is a grizzly
bear turd.

I am reminded of all the references to Indians in Harrison's
writing—friends, childhood playmates, neighbors, farmhands,
themes of Indian origin in *Wolf, A Good Day to Die,* and *Returning to Earth,* the constant hunting and fishing, the intimate con-
nections to the land, the love of animals. I want to ask Harrison
if it's true, that he is part Indian. He has dark skin, epicanthic
eyes, high cheek bones. Legend has it that when he was a student at Michigan State, hitchhiking the roads north, he used to
tell people he was part Indian. But the question remains un-
asked.

Harrison is sucking a small red lollipop, the kind you get at
banks if you're seven and you're good. He offers me some but
I decline, taking him up instead on the offer to sit in his desk
chair—the only chair in the room.

The walls of the granary are rough-sawn pine, and the wall
above his writing desk is covered with scraps of paper resem-
bling orders in a Chinese laundry; almost all are in Harrison's
large, flowing, impatient but oddly perfect and slightly femi-
nine penmanship. They are self-messages on the order of, "Remember your diet," but not that mundane. The one nearest
me says, "You must concentrate upon and consecrate yourself
wholly to each day as though a fire were raging in your hair";
these are the words of Zen master Dashimaru, Harrison says,
which formed the inspirational "code" for the two-year ordeal
of *Dalva.*

"The emotional energy I put into this book was enormous," Harrison says, adding that to create Dalva's female character he had to "totally abnegate my own personality, to become her." The book is about Dalva's search for her illegitimate son, fathered by her Indian lover, a handsome ranch hand who, unbeknownst to her, turns out to be her half-brother; this fact helps explain why she feels such a strong attraction and kinship with him, but it ultimately complicates her life and the child's.

The book opens with Dalva on a balcony on the coast of California on April 7, 1986. She is thinking of Nebraska. She is listening to the ocean and thinking of when she was baptized. Harrison says his idea for the book began involuntarily, with a vision of "this great-granddaughter standing on a balcony in Santa Monica thinking of Nebraska."

I ask Harrison what kinds of questions people have asked him about the book. "My favorite one," he says, "is, 'How did you make all this up?' I think it was a test of my talent."

Dalva has been widely reviewed and well reviewed. Jonathan Yardley at the *Washington Post* refers to Harrison as "a serious writer." The book has been popular among small groups of literati—Harrison gave a reading in New York City that was hosted by Peter Matthiessen—but the book has not yet brought Harrison the large audience Yardley said he thought Harrison would garner "if there is any such thing as literary justice."

"I realize what makes the book so impenetrable is that it's about Indians," Harrison says. "People don't know anything about the history of the country and they really don't care. But the refusal to deal with this kind of thing, this is the signatory of what's wrong with us now. Chief Seattle had a prophetic sense of this. He said, 'When you're walking in the evening and we are no longer there, we are still there.'"

Harrison points out that we killed more Indians in this country than the Nazis ever killed Jews, but that we're involved in a collective distortion of that fact. In the book, the main male character, Michael, an alcoholic professor, muses to himself that "If the Nazis had won the war the Holocaust, finally, would have been set to music, just as our victorious and bloody trek west is accompanied on film by thousands of violins and kettledrums." Harrison says that Michael can say this because he's a Falstaffian character—loud, smart, mordant, a bottom-pincher—who can get away with saying things that more serious and sympathetic characters couldn't say.

Some who've read the book say that Harrison modeled Michael after himself. Maybe so. But if that's the case then he's given Michael only his surface persona, and to Dalva herself—sensitive, smart, strong, independent, a loner—he's given his subsurface personality.

Stacked around Harrison on the floor are dozens of esoteric texts and novels sent to him by his brother, the head librarian at a university in Arkansas. One is a twelfth-century Iranian tome on falconry. Several books by Montana writer Tom McGuane line Harrison's shelves. He and McGuane met each other at Michigan State University in 1958, and the two writers have corresponded and collaborated and been good friends and hunting buddies ever since.

Harrison has been chain-smoking Marlboros and now stops to light another. "I go north in the summer," he says, indicating by way of non sequitur that we're finished. "I can't work with the noise of air conditioners." We move back out into the midday heat, which engulfs us like hot taffy.

Later I see Harrison at the Bluebird in Leland, hanging out in the bar with gentlemen my grandfather would have referred to as "some of the boys." I ask him to autograph a copy of Dalva for the friend of a friend in Denver, something I've had to do twice in the last week for people I know who know that I know Harrison. This Denver man is an attorney who slogs through legal documents ten hours a day and who has asked, therefore, for "some word of inspiration." Harrison moans and lolls his head from side to side. "Ohhhh," he says in that inimitable rasp, "Give me a break. I'm barely hanging on here." But he obliges with his signature, his one-eyed jack symbol (an eyeball that looks like a cue ball), and an Italian phrase, O chi sigura coglioni. "It's from Dante," he says. "He'll know what it means."

Later it occurs to me to try to decipher this, recruiting the help of a dozen anonymous Italian dishwashers, professors, and grandmothers. The nearest anyone can come (the spelling is in dispute) to any translation that could appear in print is, "Today for sure will be like great sex." But no one seems to think this is from Dante. Maybe not; but it is quintessential Harrison.

Living on the Land

A BLIZZARD IS RAGING outside this small, rural homestead near Cedar. It is February 1982 and this part of the country is enduring its fourth snowstorm in as many weeks.

"Come on, it's not so bad," Larry Doe tells his wife, Geradine Simkins as together they tack blankets and sheets over windows and walls on the southeast side of their house, where a fifty-mile-an-hour wind is blowing snow and icy blasts of subzero cold through invisible cracks.

"It's not so great," she answers, "when we have snow in our house."

Larry Doe and Geradine Simkins are living their beliefs.

They are doing what books such as *Muddling Toward Frugality* by Warren Johnson and *Voluntary Simplicity* by Duane Elgin say people must do if they are to survive in the twenty-first century. They are doing what the *Global 2000 Report to the President* (U.S. Department of State, 1982) says people should do if they want to stave off a worldwide resource crisis in the next twenty years. They are doing what a 1977 Louis Harris poll says two out of three Americans would like to do.

They are doing less with less. They are learning to be self-sufficient. In a benign way, they are doing what some urban folks are trying to do with the caches of guns and food: preparing to survive on their own.

If the Stanford Research Institute in Menlo Park, California, is right, people like Larry and Geradine represent about twenty percent of the population in the United States, or approximately thirty-three million adults as of the 1980 census. And if Louis Harris is right, they also represent "a quiet revolution" away from materialism.

Warren Johnson says such people are a kind of advance team for the rest of society. "If the pioneers do their work well," Johnson says, "in discovering or reviving new ways suitable for our transition to a frugal economy, and the rest of society eases in the same direction with hope and good humor, then running out of energy will no longer generate the nightmares it now does."

But being some researcher's idea of a new-age pioneer on the frontiers of social change and actually being one are two different things.

"There must have been something that build-your-own-house book from the library didn't tell me about setting in windows," Larry jokes later, in the spring, when it is okay to joke about such things. "Every time there's a strong wind from the southeast we get snow or rain in our house."

Larry, thirty-two, is a leather-worker. He spends the greater part of every day in a studio off his house stitching leather on a large, industrial sewing machine. Right now his workroom is heaped with yards and yards of butter-soft chamois suede that will be made into fancy dresses and shirts for the summer's crop of tourists who happen to visit *Ward and Eis,* a Petoskey gallery. He estimates his annual income from the leather-work, depending on the year, is between four and eight thousand dollars.

He is a man with a kind face framed by a full beard. He wears his thick brown hair shoulder length, like George Washington's in the paintings public schools usually hang above the chalkboard and under the American flag; right now it is pulled back by two yellow duck barrettes he has borrowed from his daughter Maya.

"The first person to ever see me with these duck barrettes was the UPS man," Larry says. "He brought a shipment of leather and I was so happy to see him with it I went running out into the yard and forgot all about my barrettes. After that I figured, 'what the hell.' But I take them out when I go to town."

Outside his recently completed studio is a rubble of sand, cement blocks, and old building materials. Beyond that are rolling hills where the spring sun has begun to burn through the snow to the brown earth, and what's left now looks like marble cake.

In 1977 Larry and Geradine bought the twenty acres where they live for three thousand dollars down in wedding money, a fifteen-year land contract, and monthly payments of one hundred forty-two dollars. That first summer they lived in a tent, and the snow was flying before they were inside a makeshift house that both of them sometimes refer to as a shack or a cabin. The exterior of the house has a modern, angular design; inside it is finished with barn wood and stucco and resembles a cottage in the Black Forest.

Larry built the house with salvage lumber, yard-sale hardware, a lot of gumption, and a little experience. Geradine, as they used to say in the Shake 'n' Bake ads, "halped"—when she wasn't tending to the couple's two daughters, Maya, five, and Leah, two. In order to have a steady source of income with which to buy building materials, Larry stopped doing leatherwork for the first two years they lived there and took a minimum wage job at a nearby ski resort. He estimates he has twenty-five hundred dollars hard cash in the house. The house was just recently insured for forty thousand dollars.

"I was amazed they could insure it for that much," he says. "I called them up and said, 'there must be some mistake.' They sent a guy out and he went through the whole place and they still insured it for that much."

Larry is pleased that his hard work and long hours paid off, but he says there are trade-offs. He gestures toward the building materials lying on the ground outside his studio window. "You live with materials lying around for years because you can only work in your spare time. You also learn to live with mistakes. You can't learn everything from library books. There are mis-

takes I've made on this house that would keep me awake nights, if I let them."

Larry is stirring sand on top of the wood stove in his workroom. The hot sand will be used to fill and shrink newly made replicas of eighth-century leather tankards. He says they were the forerunners of beer steins and are technically called "blackjacks." Originally produced by craftsmen in the European Guild, Larry says he believes they are now reproduced in only two places in the United States: Williamsburg, Virginia, and Greenfield Village in Detroit. Larry has researched the making of the tankards as part of a special commission from a client.

Larry is the second oldest of six children and grew up in Davison, Michigan, near Flint. He says he has always enjoyed making things and as a child liked to help his father with household projects. He attributes much of his building skill and his self-reliance to the training his father provided. Although Larry attended Michigan State on a scholarship, he dropped out after three years to become a leather-worker.

He says he was profoundly influenced by the death of his
father in 1970, when he was twenty and his father was forty-
two. "My father spent his whole life working for goals he died
too young to ever achieve. I learned from my father's death
that anything can happen at any time, and so I decided early on
that I should always do what I want to do now, before it's too
late."

"Values," Lester R. Brown writes in his new book entitled
Building a Sustainable Society, "are the key to the evolution of
society, not only because they influence behavior, but also because they determine a society's priorities and thus its ability to
survive."

Yet in Larry's case, he says it is difficult for him to know if
he is indeed part of the evolution of society's values or if, as
some of his more affluent neighbors might maintain, he is simply pulling land values down.

"Some of our neighbors," Larry says, "I think, although I
don't know this, probably see our house as an eyesore. When
they go to sell their house or their land, the value is less because
of my building materials lying around my house and my old
blue Volkswagon sitting out there in the weeds. Their parents,
on the other hand, and their grandparents who homesteaded
this land, are very encouraging. They give us vegetables out of
their garden and let us haul water from their wells and say,
'You kids are doing *fine, just fine.*' We're living the way they did
and it doesn't bother them. I myself don't know if we're a
throwback to an earlier time, or the wave of the future, or some
combination of both. I'd like to think it's the latter, or that
we're achieving a balance between the two, but I really don't
know."

Larry says he sees society becoming more and more polarized
between an ethic of materialism and its opposite. "I think of
my friends who have decided to spend their lives making
money. I haven't. I've made the opposite choice. But I guess it
disturbs me because it's like choosing up sides. Now we're on
opposite sides of the battle. But it's not as clear-cut as a battle.
It's more subtle than that."

In a chapter entitled "Civilization in Transition," in *Voluntary Simplicity,* Duane Elgin writes that American society is in a critical state of change. "A wartime psychology prevails," he says, "but it is a war without a visible opponent. In reality we are at war with ourselves and our fear of the unknown challenge that lies beyond the industrial era." It is not a war that is being fought in the streets, but rather one that is being fought in the hearts and minds of the people and in the way they live and conduct their lives.

"It's like we're all part of some Darwinian experiment," Larry sums up, "and we just don't know yet which group is going to evolve in the direction of survival: the old-fashioned seekers of the American dream of money, or the new-fashioned seekers of a more humanitarian and spiritual American dream."

It is pretty where the Doe-Simkins live. Even during one of the coldest springs in memory, the hills are graceful and pleasing to the eye. It is a landscape reminiscent of that in a J. R. R. Tolkien story, the kind of setting where one expects to see a troop of elves come marching gaily down the road singing, "Over hill, over dale . . ." on their way to some noble adventure.

When the sun sets in these hills—over in the west where the clouds roll and bank over Lake Michigan—it creates a kaleidoscope of a fuchsia and peach and cerise and orange and crimson sky for thirty minutes or more. Yet even the rosiest glow from the loveliest sunset doesn't exactly create a daily idyll.

For three years the family lived without a well on their land. Instead, they hauled water from the neighbors' well and didn't take a lot of baths. In the winter, when their quarter-mile-long driveway is impassable, this meant carrying forty-pound drums of water, uphill, every other day on a toboggan.

Even now, in the winter, everything else—propane, groceries, two children too small to walk—has to be hauled up the driveway. Geradine is a midwife and on winter nights when she is called out to attend a birth she must navigate the long driveway on foot, sometimes through waist-deep snow drifts and sometimes with Maya on a sled and Leah in a backpack. Geradine is short, five feet and no more, and it's a trek that would daunt many a six-footer—without the kids.

"We wait for the hard crust snow in March," Larry says, "we can walk on top of that. But then in April there's mud. We can't bring the car up in that either, unless we do it early in the morning after a hard frost. In summer it's okay, but in the fall it gets muddy again if we have a lot of rain."

Together Larry and Geradine are helping Maya and Leah make bread. Maya is making a fruit-basket, and Leah is making doughy, whole wheat balls she calls babies. Leah's "babies" have little flecks of something in them that Larry finally determines to be blue PlayDoh.

"What we have," Geradine says, "is a lot of hard work and some deprivation, offset by almost unlimited freedom and control over our own lives. We don't punch a time clock or work for a boss. We don't have weeks, or weekends. We can follow the natural rhythms of the seasons and of our own intuitive sense of things. There's an exhilarating sense of personal power that comes from living here, but there's also a lot of personal responsibility." She tilts her head to the side. "Sometimes I think we must be crazy to live this way—especially in winter—but deep down I know it's the only right way."

It is a life-style that is looking better and better as times get harder and harder, Larry Doe says, pointing out that people everywhere are losing their jobs, their homes, and their businesses. In Michigan, where unemployment ranges between twelve and twenty-five percent, depending on the area and the time of year, everyone knows someone who is laid off. He cites a recent *Newsweek* article that says that in the United States as a whole between 1980 and 1981, mortgage foreclosures increased by thirty-one percent, business failures by forty-five percent, and bankruptcies by eleven percent.

But the Doe-Simkins believe they are only minimally affected by the U.S. economy. They have no debts and, other than a $142 a month land contract payment, no mortgages. They are self-employed and so do not have to worry about losing a job. They grow their own food and so are only slightly affected by inflated prices at the grocery store. They heat with wood and so fuel costs are not a major concern. Larry does his own auto repairs, and with yard sales, thrift shops, and sewing, Geradine provides the family with clothing and household needs. They belong to a food co-op and barter for many goods and services. They pay three hundred dollars a year in property taxes and no income tax.

"There's a lot of security in knowing you're so far below the poverty line you don't have to worry about getting any poorer," Larry says.

When the ice goes out and the birds come back, then people in northern Michigan begin to socialize again. Tonight is March 21, the spring equinox, the time when the sun rises precisely in the east and sets precisely in the west, a time when the day and the night, the length of light and dark, will be exactly the same—and Larry and Geradine are having some friends in to celebrate. She is cooking something that looks like it will be refried beans and cheese nachos covered with chopped green onion and tomatoes, and as she cooks she talks.

"The thing I have given up to live here," she says, "is the security of belonging to the mainstream, the security of being viewed as normal."

She talks about her neighborhood in Dearborn Heights where she grew up. She was the oldest of four children. "I was always with a bunch of kids, always organizing something. We'd go on a picnic to the park and pretend we were all orphans. Or we'd put on a play. We were always doing crazy things that were fun." Later, she says, at the Catholic, all-girl Holy Rosary High School in downtown Detroit, she was a member of the student council, a class officer, and a good student.

She says she began to change from what she calls a middle-class life-style when she was ten and John F. Kennedy was running for president. "I organized all the kids in my neighborhood into this huge marching band with tin pans and spoons

and a large banner that said, 'Vote for J.F.K.' and we toured
Dearborn Heights. I was young and didn't know much, but it
seemed that Kennedy stood for something more than other
presidents had: something human, or hopeful, or caring. And I
suppose I could relate to the fact that he was Catholic." Her
father, at that time a Nixon fan and a Republican, was embar-
rassed by the commotion Geradine made in the neighborhood,
and he took her banner out of the garage and burned it. Later
he apologized and he and Geradine's mother would become
what Geradine calls "more socially aware" and "actually lead
the way for me to become more aware."

In the 1960s, Geradine says, Pope John XXIII issued a papal
encyclical that said, in essence, that all Catholics should begin
to live more like Christ. "My parents took this seriously, and
so did I." By the time Geradine was in her third year at Wayne
State University she had decided, she says, "there was more to
learn outside of school than in school." She abandoned her plans
to become a teacher and instead joined an antiwar group called
the Detroit Peace Collective. She wrote speeches, and she gave
speeches; she went on national speaking tours and protest
marches and generally worked to end the war in Vietnam. In
1972 she decided she needed a personal life. She moved north
to Traverse City where she met Larry.

"We discovered we both wanted the same things: a little farm
in the country, children, marriage, and a life doing work we
liked, which for Larry was leather-work and for me at that time
was creative sewing. It was a fantasy but it seemed like one we
could achieve."

It turned out to be harder than either of them had ever
dreamed. "We learned that you can't be a craftsman and have a
middle-class life-style. It takes a lot of work, a lot of self-disci-
pline, and there's very little money in it." To this day the Doe-
Simkins family has no health insurance, no life insurance, no
pension plan, no Social Security benefits, and, at their income
level, no way to save for their retirement.

The alleged thirty-three million persons who are living in a
deliberately unmaterialistic manner are described by the Stan-

ford Research Institute as *inner-directed consumers.* "These are people," the researchers say, "who are often younger persons (members of the post-World-War-II-baby-boom-generation) from middle-class backgrounds who are relatively well-educated. Inner-directed consumers tend to be idealistic, spiritually inclined, ecologically oriented, and experimental in their manner of living. Members of this group consume according to their inner sense of what is appropriate, rather than relying on prevailing fashion or the expectations of others as their primary guide."

Unlike *need-driven consumers,* who mainly want to know where their next meal is coming from, and unlike *outer-directed consumers,* who worry a lot about what other people think of them, the *inner-directed consumers,* according to the Stanford researchers, are unconcerned about the opinions of others.

Geradine disagrees.

"It bothers me a lot," she says, "to be poor. I still haven't gotten used to it. It's not the way I was raised. It also causes me a great deal of anxiety to realize I'm so far removed from the path of my high school friends.

"My dream," she says, "is not to be isolated out in the country, but to experience the commonality of the human spirit. And I'm not living out here because I'm afraid of the bomb dropping or don't want to live in cities. I certainly don't see any virtue in poverty. In a way I guess I'd like to go back to the middle class because it would bring me closer to the majority of people again. But for me personally, to give up this way of life would mean that I'm not psychologically strong enough to do it. For me, this is the way of survival of the future."

Geradine has been chopping onions furiously as she talks.

She is Irish, second generation, and right now she looks particularly Irish as her thick, hip-length braid of reddish-brown hair sways back and forth as she talks.

"People who are initiators and self-motivators are going to survive," she says. "People who are dependent on the culture the way it is now are going to be utterly lost. The people who survive are going to be the people who know how to grow their own food, create their own jobs, provide their own health care, educate their kids, and get along with other people. This is lost information. These are survival skills we all used to have that we just don't have a handle on any more."

The people who come for dinner that night are perhaps as good a reflection of Larry and Geradine as anything else might be. Lori Cruden is a midwife who supports herself and her six-year-old son, Gabriel, with the proceeds from her mail-order herb garden business. Rick Jones is a Tennessee hillbilly and a sculptor of unicorns and wood sprites. He was recently a guest artist in an "Artists in the Schools" program. His wife, Carol, is a speech pathologist. They are all in their late twenties or early thirties.

On the whole they are artistic, pantheistic, humanistic, and highly independent in their thinking. There seems to be an unstated agreement among them that they form a kind of extended family, a community, the beginnings of a new society. They resemble, as much as anything else, the descendants of the people who came over on the *Mayflower*. They would be recognized anywhere in the world as Americans.

That night around a bonfire, they celebrate the beginning of spring, the return of the birds, and friendship.

"We are here tonight," Geradine says as she tells everyone to hold hands, "to be together and eat and thank God for bringing the warm weather back—sooner please."

In a book called simply, *Families,* former *Life* magazine staffer Jane Howard points out that a family can be any group of people who are independent and who, especially, "enliven their lives with ritual."

"The best families I know," she writes, "are the ones who celebrate the ceremonies that link people to the earth, to those who have trod it before them, and to one another." And that, in a way, is what the bonfire is all about: a linking to the earth and to the people who have trod it before.

"These are times of intense change," Geradine says, "but we must not stop there and dig into depression. We have to see these times as a wonderful opportunity for renewal and rebirth of the human potential."

One Saturday afternoon about a week later there is a gray, March rain falling outside. Water runs down the driveway in small streams and sluices. An old Gene Kelly movie, *Brigadoon,* is playing on TV.

It is hard to find simple solutions to complex problems, but the mythical town of Brigadoon, in Scotland, has succeeded. Long years ago, so the story goes, the town's pastor decided the world was becoming too nasty a place for his people. And so he sent a special prayer heavenward that all the people in the town of Brigadoon would fall asleep that night, and when they woke up again it would be a hundred years later. He prayed that one whole day and night in the town of Brigadoon would be a hundred years in the rest of the world. And in the meantime Brigadoon would be enveloped in a thick mist that would part only once in every hundred years so that it and the rest of the world could get a glimpse of each other. This way, so the theory went, the town would never be exposed to evil long enough to be changed by it.

"This is a perfect day for *Brigadoon,*" Geradine says as she watches the mist fill the little valley between her house and the rise of hills to the south of it.

Geradine has been singing along with Gene Kelly to the tune of "Bonnie Jean," and "The Heather on the Hill," and dancing barefoot in front of the TV, her long hair swaying. "Did you know I could dance all these old Irish dances?" she asks her husband.

"Yes, Geradine. I know."

For the time being, Geradine says, it seems as though their family, like the town of Brigadoon, has escaped from the out-side world. Yet, she says, the doubt persists: are they simply living beyond the pale or are they part of some as yet undis-closed brave new world? She turns to her husband, "Which is it, Larry?"

"I don't know," he says. "Maybe we'll have to wait another one hundred years for the mist to part again."

Upon Accepting an Invitation to Listen to a Tape in Leland

IN THE PAST YEAR I have been invited to "listen to a tape" at least eight times. So isolated are we here on this northern peninsula, I can't tell if this is some new fad sweeping the country or if it is a strictly local custom, an aspect of living in a region so faraway and antipodean that we don't get actual speakers, only tapes of speakers.

On the occasion of this writing, in the early spring of 1984, I am sitting on a nubby tweed sofa in a little house on a little back street in Leland, on the Leelanau Peninsula, listening to the disembodied voice of Sonia Johnson, the female candidate for president, come out of a black tape recorder on the other side of an Oriental carpet.

About a dozen women are here with me. There's a social worker, a bookkeeper, a business manager, a librarian, a physical therapist, a medical assistant, a quilt crafter, a carpenter, a teacher, a clothing-store owner, and a secretary—all sitting around this tastefully appointed house sipping white wine spritzers and nibbling tamari rice crackers.

For about the first five minutes, there is a huge bump on the tape that creates a sound like a stick being dragged over a rubber threshold. The tape is obviously worn from many playings, and I can't help but think, as I stare out the window at the forsythia in bloom, that this cloistered group of women in this pin-dot village on the shores of Lake Michigan—two hundred eighty miles from Detroit and three thousand miles from San Francisco, where Sonia Johnson first gave this speech in September 1983—is not too different from some tucked away pocket of villagers in the Himalayas; and that this tape is not unlike some year-old letter that's been passed from village to village and read so many times that it's nearly worn through.

A carillon chimes somewhere up the hill, and Sonia says, *"We know the most unifying thing in the women's movement is the hatred of Reagan. He is the enemy. He represents the patriarchy that's been trying to kill women for four thousand years."* The woman across the room is nodding and smiling. A woman sitting next to the plate of dilled brussels sprouts is listening with hands folded, like a schoolgirl.

I realize I know little about Sonia Johnson except that she was excommunicated by the Mormon church for her support of the Equal Rights Amendment. I have come to this gathering because I am curious and because the kids have chicken pox and I needed to get out of the house. The sun is setting over Lake Michigan, and Sonia is saying, "Eighteen-month-old baby girls are being treated for syphilis of the throat . . . fifty percent of women in relationships with men are beaten . . . and you think we're not at war? What do you think war is?"

The tape is not over a moment when Sonia Johnson's district coordinator, a clothing-store owner from Beaulah, is on her feet saying, "We're talking about a truly revolutionary change on the planet. CBS and NBC have told her to call them up if she gets a hundred thousand dollars (in donations). If she gets even one minute on national TV, she'll blow their minds, because she's not going to talk about getting out of El Salvador, she's going to talk about *women*."

The district coordinator says Johnson has raised almost fifty thousand dollars of the one hundred thousand dollars she needs to qualify for matching federal funds. Then she says something about how endemic male oppression is. "I don't like to be afraid when I jog at night," she says.

Women start getting out their checkbooks. "I expected to be inspired and I was," says the business manager. "I thought she was *wonderful*," says the lady carpenter. "I became aware of the violence against women when I worked as a rape counselor," says the social worker. A couple of women say something about "too polarized," or "too much emphasis on hate," but they are in the minority. "What I liked," says the physical therapist, "was that she represents all people, not just women."

Those who liked the tape seemed to like it because they liked Sonia Johnson, and, above all, because they liked the idea of a female candidate. Those who didn't like the tape knew little about Sonia Johnson, but also liked the idea of a female candidate. There was a little eddy of tension immediately after the tape shut off when it appeared there might be some difference of opinion about Sonia's qualifications for president, but this evaporated as women steered toward the food and other topics of conversation.

I am puzzled by the tape. Puzzled by the response to it. I write out a check for five dollars (I feel I owe something for my tamari rice cracker and my place on the sofa, and I basically support anybody's right to matching funds), and I leave.

Outside a gray-yellow twilight sits on the streets. Leland is not Alaska, but it is far enough north that even at ten o'clock at night in the summer the sky is still light. As I walk up the sidewalk to my car I am thinking not about getting mugged by a member of the patriarchy, but about those old paper towel commercials on TV, the "quicker picker upper" ads. I used to love to watch how the liquid spill would spread out from the center and make small, random paths, fading to the outer edges. I decide that's where we are in Leland. We are so far from the center that we can't even tell—on the basis of some year-old, edited, very worn, and scratchy tape—what was spilled. Dim awareness arrives in our area, just at that moment when Nancy Walker used to say, "The quicker picker upper, folks."

New Yorkers on the Leelanau

WHEN MANHATTANITES start moving into the midwestern backwaters, into a nowhere northern Michigan peninsula like the Leelanau, you know something's happening to the country's demographics. It's too soon to say what, but the feeling you have watching it is similar to seeing geese flying north in November: it's not what you expect.

In the spring of 1987 a friend came back from a business trip and said he'd sat next to a man on the plane who was commuting between Leland, where he lived, and New York, where he had a factory. Then in the late fall of 1987 I went to a town meeting in Glen Arbor (population one hundred fifty), and a former New York journalist came in and sat down next to me and began commenting dryly, with broad *a*'s, on the proceedings.

We've had New Yorkers in here before, but they usually left. There was the guy down in Empire a few years ago who brought his Manhattan bride home to live above the dry-goods store. That union of opposites lasted about six months—March is the hard season here—before she returned to a place where, as she said, she could at least go shopping.

Someone once said that if the Leelanau Peninsula has a polar opposite, it's probably Manhattan. People from there don't just wander in here and last; the culture shock is too great.

But this group of people from New York coming into the Leelanau Peninsula now aren't people who just ended up here by mistake—like one stray goose that got separated from the flock. Nor do they resemble the back-to-the-land folks of the seventies or the steady trickle of summer resorters from Detroit and Chicago who retire up here. These newcomers are seekers, true pioneers, and, as such, they have more in common with the first wave of immigrants to this peninsula a century ago.

I can say this because I went around and talked to some of them. This peninsula has a population of only about fifteen thousand, and it is possible, just by knowing a lot of people, to be aware of a trend—even if it's not charted statistically.

Dayton Spence is an artist from Manhattan, and I heard about him long before I met him. He came to do restoration work on the Traverse City Opera House and decided to stay and live in Suttons Bay. Because he works all over the United States, he can live anywhere.

One day I talked to him in his lakeshore studio. Although originally from Detroit, he moved to New York in 1975 and lived there until coming to the Leelanau Peninsula in 1987. He tells me he did restoration work at the Helmsley Palace in New York, at the Waldorf Astoria, and on the John LaFarge murals.

Locally he heads the architectural restoration division of Burdco, a Traverse City–based company. He is a tall, red-headed man, outgoing, a talker.

"I love it here," Spence says. "It's calm. I feel my life changed when I came here. It has a frontier quality, but every day I'm surprised at the sophistication. I met Jim Harrison, the writer, artists Ben Brown and David Grath. There's a world–class talent here. I'd like to do a gallery just to showcase what's here."

Bob Hennelly is one of those people with a Renaissance man résumé: classical dancer, Ford Foundation fellow, prize–winning reporter, detective, speech writer for Jesse Jackson, arts administrator for the National Academy for the Arts. I first learned about him after reading one of his free-lance concert reviews in the local paper. On the phone he tells me he lived in

New York and New Jersey all his life before moving to the Leelanau Peninsula. He says he couldn't even drive when he first moved out of Manhattan because he'd always taken public transportation. Now he lives in a nineteenth-century homestead near the village of Northport with his wife, Lisa, and a new baby.

It is late afternoon when I arrive at the Hennelly home. Lisa is about to go to her job making pizzas at a local bar, and Bob is just coming home from his job in a Northport woodworking shop. The couple recently bought this house, barn, and twenty acres for $34,900, something Bob says they never could have done back East, where one-eighth of an acre with nothing on it sells for $50,000. He and Lisa met in Bergen County, New Jersey. She was working there as a governess, after having answered a newspaper ad back in Michigan for a governess with "fundamental Midwest values." Bob was working as a reporter for the *Ridgewood News*. They came back here to Northport, where Lisa was from, after they got married.

"One day when we came home back East, there was a note on our door from the New Jersey Health Department saying there were seventy-two contaminants in our water and we might want to start buying bottled water at the store," Lisa says. Bob adds, "I was doing a story on toxic waste, homes being built on landfills. I was aware from my research that the whole area was poisonous."

I ask Lisa what was meant by "fundamental Midwest values." She says she didn't know, but it seemed to mean "someone who wouldn't steal their jewels and who would take care of their kids." She said the people she worked for were gone all the time. "The boy became so attached to me, he'd walk in his sleep and think I was his mother; when he'd wake up and find out I wasn't, he'd fly into a violent rage. I was afraid I was going to get hurt." She worked for two families and both seemed to neglect the emotional needs of their children, something she attributes to what she sees as the importance of making money in the East.

"They didn't get their identity from their families, but from their careers and how much money they made," she says. "I'd never want to raise kids there."

Bob says he misses reporting and the variety of people in New York, but thinks he will find community and opportunity on the Leelanau Peninsula.

Bev Gilmore is the fashionably dressed journalist who sat next to me in the Glen Arbor town meeting. Now—over lunch in Leland—I learn she was the trend editor of the *Staten Island Advance* for fifteen years. "I'd talk to Bill Blass on the phone in the morning," she says, "see a Perry Ellis show in the afternoon. I miss it." Gilmore says she became deathly ill while on assignment in Tokyo. When she returned to Manhattan, the pneumonialike disease was diagnosed as an allergic reaction to pollution. The allergic reaction was triggered by the excessive pollution in Tokyo, Gilmore says, and exacerbated by the pollution in Manhattan. She was treated by Dr. Marshall Mandell, director of the Center for Bio-Ecologic Disease in Norwalk, Connecticut, who advised her to leave New York City. She decided to come north to Michigan's Leelanau Peninsula, where her sister had a condominium at The Homestead.

"My life was everything you think of as New York," she says. "I loved my job and I was very good at it. I loved the competition and I loved being successful. That's why it's so tough to have this illness and not be able to be there, where everything is. But this peninsula has been a miracle for me. A year ago I couldn't get out of bed.

"I don't know how to characterize a city ... as finite?" Gilmore says. "But the opposite of that is here; this is infinite. New York City is a construct. New York is the center of the universe—just ask Mayor Koch. And people in New York really believe that." Later she writes me a letter and says, "As much as New York is intellect, Glen Arbor is spirit. I don't ever expect to tire of watching the changing surface patterns, textures, and colors of water, dunes, and islands."

Natural beauty, clean air and water, and something as intangible as "fundamental Midwest values" have brought New

Yorkers to this peninsula; they have come out of the city not, as the early pioneers, for the promise of frontier adventure, virgin timber, or other untold riches, but simply for the basics—breathable air and drinkable water.

That's a major change and something that would have been inconceivable thirty years ago when I was growing up here. I remember the senior trip the Empire High School Class of '53 took to New York City, and the giddiness that was felt throughout our small school, even in my third-grade class, at the thought of those six seniors staying in a hotel, with a doorman, and eating in a restaurant. Then, Manhattan was the Big Apple—although I don't think it was called that yet; this peninsula, which barely existed in the mind of the rest of the world, was definitely small potatoes.

The world has contracted since the 1950s. People go to Katmandu and Manhattan, and people come here. TV, not to mention planes, takes us everywhere. The global population has doubled since the 1950s, from 2.5 billion to 5 billion. If it doubles again in the next 30 years, we'll be lucky if we can even grow potatoes on the peninsula, let alone *be* potatoes, small or otherwise.

The Sleeping Bear Dunes
and
the Shifting Sands of
Bureaucracy

CANTILEVERED OUT OVER the bluff is a deck like the crow's nest on a ship. Standing there on a spring night in 1979, one feels placed at the top of the world.

Richard Quick finished building this deck, in front of his home near the northern Michigan village of Glen Arbor, just before the federal government declared in 1970 that Quick's deck—and his home and the forty acres around it and about seventy thousand more acres belonging to other people—were going to become a national park.

"Congress finds," the act reads, "that certain outstanding natural features, including forests, beaches, dune formations, and ancient glacial phenomena, exist along the mainland shores of Lake Michigan and on certain nearby islands in Leelanau County, Michigan."

From his deck Quick can see all of Sleeping Bear Bay. Starting from the buff-colored tip of the dunes in the southwest and sweeping around to the sharp peaks of evergreen at Pyramid Point in the northeast, it is a view of breathtaking proportions, encompassing two emerald green islands—North and South Manitou—in a bay of Lake Michigan as blue as the Mediterranean.

"Those islands do something for you," Quick says, softly. "They come and go. It's awful pretty when ships come through there all lit up at night." He says he will not move, although he knows that he is in the path of federal takeover. "I have ninety-seven birch trees and thirteen deer who come to my backyard. It would be wasteful for me to move, with the beauty I have here."

Quick, who was born and raised in Glen Arbor, has loved the place where his home is since he was thirteen; he "discovered it one day, and just couldn't get enough of it, and kept coming back."

Although he owns one of the most spectacular pieces of property in the county, Quick did not come by it easily. Following a hitch in the Army, he returned to Glen Arbor, opened a gas station, saved his money, and worked for the day when he would be able to build his own home. At forty-four, he says he is just beginning to "get it the way I want it."

Now the government wants it too, but Quick says no. "I will fight them every step of the way. They'll have to get a court order just to come on my property to appraise it." His fierce stand is well known to his neighbors. However, he does not sound fierce now as he says, "All I want is to die there. But they don't understand the feelings I have."

Quick is not alone in thinking that "they"—meaning the federal government—do not understand his strong feelings of attachment for the land he lives on. Nor is it conceivable to local people that the tourists will understand or ever achieve the strong feelings that the local people have for their duneland. It is incomprehensible to people born and raised in Glen Arbor that throngs of summer visitors—people in Winnebagos, people from Ohio or Florida or Maine, who come for a day or a week—will ever understand the daily rhythms and moods of the place where they grew up, a land that is part of them and they of it, a land for which their feelings are so close to the bone that it is almost impossible, if not improper, for them to be articulated.

How does one begin to tell someone that they don't want to move from the dunes because the stars there are closer to the earth than anywhere else in the world? Or that the quality of light on a clear day in mid-August brings the Manitous so close to the mainland that it seems one could reach out and touch them? Or how, in the spring when the ice has gone out of the bay and you are walking home from a baseball game in Glen Arbor, the air smells so thick with pine and arbutus that every breath you take seems to blend you with it?

People seldom, if ever, talk that way to strangers about the place they live. The closest they come to saying anything like "love" is: "We were taking care of it before they came. We don't need them to take care of it for us."

This argument—heard often at meetings—has an emotional and childish ring to it, and outsiders can defeat it in a moment merely by pointing to instances where local people did not "take care of it" before the park was created.

"People said they were taking care of it," says a businessman who moved to Glen Arbor just as the park was taking shape, "but I can walk a hundred yards back in the woods and find garbage dumps. Huge cans of oil and old car parts. If that is the way people were taking care of it, then I'd rather have the National Park Service take care of it. Personally I think the park is the greatest thing that ever happened to this little spot on earth. Without it, this place would have been another Aspen in ten or twenty years. I'm all for keeping it a wilderness, or so-called wilderness."

Nonetheless, people do live in these seventy-one thousand acres that the government declared a "wilderness," and as one former park superintendent, Julius Martinek, observes, "Some of the wildest animals in the park are the people who've lived there for three generations." Settlers, homesteaders, Indians— they are as much a part of the natural life on the land as the rabbits and deer the park was created to protect.

"I was born right here," says Labon Vandenhoof, one of the

few Indians in the park. "I didn't just move in. I can remember when that road in front of my place was a two-track." Vandenhoof says that the government has always taken land away from the Indians and now they are doing it to everyone.

Vandenhoof claims that he was paid only half of what his land was worth, in spite of a court battle for fair value. "I don't think you could describe what it's like to fight the government," he says. "They're all crooks. They lies to you too much."

The battle between the individual property owner and the government is described as "unequal" by attorney Ken Thompson, who has represented landholders since the late sixties. The government definitely has things weighted in its favor, Thompson observes, because "the government has unlimited resources and is, of course, immortal. The sheer expense and weight of litigation will defeat the individual property owner."

Thompson, a dry-eyed observer of this battle since it began, says: "People don't understand, simply cannot comprehend, the awesome power of the government taking private property. People talk about rights, but really that never gets to be an issue. Once you've lost the legislative battle, the only argument is whether or not you've gotten fair value."

Not everyone decides to fight for fair value. Some, like seventy-year-old Lila Hunter, have neither the time nor the money nor the energy nor, simply, enough years left in their lives to take on the government. "They were after me like a bumblebee until I let them have that back property," she says. "Now I hope they leave me alone until I die." She still has her house and barn and three acres and neither delusions nor bitterness about the fact that she was taken by the government. "They'll cheat you if they think they can get away with it, and you can't fight them," she says, and then adds, for balance: "Of course, there is a difference in where the land lies. But there shouldn't be twice as much difference."

Thompson's comment on this is: "It's the obligation of the government employee not to pay any more for property than he is legally required to. Anything more would be a waste of taxpayers' money and would subject the employee to criticism."

The superintendent of the park, Don Brown, explains it a little differently: "The impression people have is that this is the federal government, and you have, you know, unlimited resources. This really is not the case. In fact, we're entering now into a time of real austerity."

As reasonable or unreasonable as this might sound, depending on which side one wishes to take, an individual trying to get "fair value" and deal with the bureaucracy can soon feel overwhelmed. Delores Wilcox, a single parent with five children to raise, an eighty-seven-year-old grandfather to look after, a yearly income of six thousand dollars, and an order from the Park Service that she must vacate her trailer adjacent to her grandfather's house, says: "I can't afford a lawyer, but I can't afford not to have one either."

Having already moved once because of the park, Mrs. Wilcox is now faced with having to move again. As she explains her predicament, it is obvious she has been over and over this ground many times before: "I can't replace what I have for the money they'll give me. So I will not only be forced to move, but be forced into debt.

"They would treat me as a tenant and let me lease my home back until 1983, but I've still got kids in school at that time. Grandpa is eligible for relocation allotment—fifteen thousand dollars—but he doesn't want to move. If I have tenant status, I'm not eligible for relocation money. And the park wants to consider me a tenant, even though I own the land with Grandpa. They won't give me more than nine thousand dollars for my trailer. I can't replace it or move for that. They'll give Grandpa twenty-four thousand dollars for the house. Both of them are worth more with the land.

"Grandpa doesn't want to move, so I would have to find a place close by. One of the big things is that there is no reasonable property available anywhere in the county, much less close by. And I don't know what to look for, because I don't know how much they'll give me or what the legal fees will be. So I can't make a down payment on anything.

"None of this takes into account that I've been used to sitting here looking down the road toward Glen Arbor, watching the deer cross the road, for nigh onto thirty years. I'm on a main road that's plowed regularly. I'm a mile and a half from work. Further, the trailer can't really be moved because it's too small for the rezoning. The only place you can move a trailer is way back off the road, which leaves a lot to be desired in the middle of winter.

"When it gets right down to it, it's quite a thing to try to figure out what you're going to do."

Brown seems to recognize this pitfall for landowners. "We try to listen to people, to be responsive within the limitations of the bureaucracy—which are awesome—but there is often so much red tape that people become exhausted simply trying to hack through it."

Although Brown is considered to be a vast improvement over his predecessor and to be "reasonably decent" and "making an effort," according to people who have had dealings with him, he is described by Vandenhoof as "a man who tries to play it cool. He talks a good game, but when you come right down to it, he's a puppet."

Brown is an enigma to landholders Kathy and Tom Stocklin. Kathy says: "I can't quite decide which side he's on. I guess mainly I feel sorry for him. I think he's basically an honorable man, or was before he took this job, but it disturbs me to hear him tell us one thing one day and another thing the next. He has bosses over him, I know that. Sometimes I wonder how he can sleep at night. I see him fighting his conscience. I think he's a tormented man."

Brown's counterpart in the park bureaucracy is Jim Williamson, head of the land acquisition office. If Brown is "the good guy," then Williamson is "the bad guy" in the minds of most people who have had dealings with the Park Service.

Williamson, a former bomber pilot, has the job of "actually

acquiring the land," he explains in a Southern accent. It isn't a job designed to increase anyone's popularity, and Vandenhoof says, "Williamson ain't walking healthy in this county."

However, Williamson himself says, "I don't think I'm really unpopular," and adds that he likes his job because it enables him to "come into contact with many different kinds of people."

As for taking people's land away from them, Williamson says: "You have empathy, but it's like the Doc saying, 'I'm going to cut off your leg.' Land is a very emotional thing for many people. You can see that from history, the great lengths people will go to get land. So when you take their land you touch a very sensitive nerve. But it's not me [taking the land]. I mean, Congress has spoken, and I'm just carrying out Congressional orders."

The team of Brown and Williamson makes the Stocklins feel like "we're being steamrollered, because while Brown is working and cooperating with us, Williamson goes around the back way and condemns us."

The Stocklins, who own a canoe livery within the park boundaries, never anticipated that their land would be condemned, because they have a certificate from the Secretary of Interior saying that it wouldn't be.

So when it happened, "we were dumbfounded," Kathy Stocklin says. Her husband adds that "what really bothers us is we didn't buy this property and then get the letter prohibiting condemnation. We got the letter first, and then bought the property." Tom worked for Dupont Chemical in South Carolina and Kathy taught school there before they came to northern Michigan. They are both thirty-three. All their savings are in their business. "This land is not just our home, it's our only source of income," says Tom Stocklin.

According to the act creating the national park, the Stocklins' canoe livery falls into the category of "compatible use" and supposedly wouldn't be condemned even if there were no letter from the Secretary of the Interior saying it wouldn't be.

One reason they gave up good jobs and plunked down their savings on the canoe livery was that it was in the national park and "seemed like a stable income." They are sure they will never find another canoe livery on another river in another national park—"how many national parks are there?"—even if the government did give them "fair value."

They are "afraid we are going to be railroaded into condemnation proceedings before we get our questions answered." Both complain of headaches and jitters. Kathy says she still shakes with rage and fear every time she remembers the day "Williamson came in while Tom was in Traverse getting supplies. I was waiting on a customer. He threw his briefcase up on the glass counter—I thought it was going to shatter—and demanded to appraise us then or he was going to condemn us. It wasn't a request—it was a threat."

The Stocklins are suing the federal government for "breach of promise" and "intimidation through lack of due process." They have no money; all their money is in their business. However, the Stocklins, like Mrs. Wilcox, can't afford not to have a lawyer.

"We are very much in favor of this park, and have been since the beginning," Tom Stocklin says. "But we don't feel people should be taken advantage of in the process. The thing is, I guess I never thought the government would do this. Unless it happens to you, you don't believe it can."

The Stocklins aren't the only ones suing the government. The Sleeping Bear Dunes Citizens' Council, an organization formed in 1974 to protect the rights of people in the park, is suing the government for "purposefully giving special treatment to those property owners who express a willingness to waive their constitutional rights to just compensation . . . guaranteed under the Fifth Amendment . . . and who make a gift of their property in exchange for special treatment. . . ." The suit is presently in federal court in Grand Rapids.

The practice is widespread enough to be readily acknowledged by Department of the Interior employee Bob Herbst. In a letter dated November 9, 1978, Herbst writes to explain: "The owner offered to donate 11.26 of the tract's 12.48 acres and to sell the remaining 1.22 acres, containing the residence, to the

National Park Service if permitted to use and occupy the residence for the remainder of his life. The net result was that the National Park Service acquired for seventy-one thousand thirty dollars, property that was appraised at two hundred thirty thousand dollars. The savings to taxpayers, and the fact that development and management objectives at the lakeshore were not adversely affected, dictated the acceptance of the offer."

The government practice of "deliberately jumping around in purchasing and leaving the purchase of large holdings until last, leaving the owner the right to pay taxes and be a caretaker, nearly broke many people," says Arthur Huey, one of the largest landowners in the park. Although this practice did not break him, it significantly limited his development.

Huey says that the management of the park is vastly improved since Brown took over. He describes the earlier managers as "politically naive" and "riding roughshod over people" when it would have been easier for them and better in the long run to be more diplomatic with local residents. "People felt the heavy foot of government in this area," Huey says, although lately, he adds, the Park Service has "made an effort to be more responsive to the needs of the community."

Brown says he has made a deliberate attempt to do this, instigating such things as reimbursement to local fire departments. Before Brown did this, local fire departments were expected to patrol the lakeshore, where there were more people than ever before, with fewer tax dollars.

"I want to see if we can meet the needs of the general public and still meet the needs of the local people," Brown says repeatedly. And according to attorney Thompson, this is the crux of the dunes issue. All other things notwithstanding—legal suits, individual gripes, and governmental concerns—"the real issue," Thompson says, "is the conflict between the private right to own land and the public right to parks."

The Sleeping Bear Dunes National Lakeshore probably wouldn't exist today, most agree, if it were not for the late Michigan Senator Philip Hart. Hart's son, Walter, who sits on the Sleeping Bear Dunes Advisory Board, says: "Our family does understand the many sacrifices people have made for this park."

Many people, even those who "felt the heavy foot of government," as Art Huey says, feel as he does: "The park is here. Now what I want is to see this become the best national park in the country."

Reservation Gambling

DOWN THE ROAD from me on the Leelanau Peninsula is one of the few gambling casinos west of Atlantic City and east of Nevada. The Leelanau Sands Casino, one of the newer business ventures of the Grand Traverse Band of Ottawa and Chippewa Indians, sits halfway up a hill on the reservation next to the Bingo Palace. Both overlook Grand Traverse Bay.

One day in the long rainy spring of 1986, I decided to go over and see what it was like to play bingo and gamble. I had always wanted to see what the Bingo Palace looked like, and because I've never been in a casino, I wanted to see that too.

The village of Peshawbestown is about twenty-five miles north of Traverse City on M-22. There's a gas station, a motel, an Indian art store, a church, the new tribal administration buildings, the Bingo Palace, and the casino.

The Sunday afternoon I visit, the four-hundred-fifty-seat Bingo Palace is about half full. I don't know what I had expected to find inside—raucous laughter, conversation, high spirits—but I am unprepared for what I do find. The place is quiet and has an almost hypnotic torpor, with the bingo caller announcing, "I-19, B-11" and so on, all through the sleepy afternoon. A young Indian girl pushes a cart up and down the aisles calling, "jar tickets," like a hot dog vendor at a circus, but even she is subdued. Almost all of the players are older women. There appear to be about a dozen Indian young people working here. A few adult Indians are playing bingo, but not many.

Most of the women say they play bingo to forget their problems. They like "the Palace" because they say the young workers are nice and the place is clean. Some come early to socialize and buy lunch from the concession stand that offers blanket dogs, Indian tacos, fry bread, soda pop, and coffee. The Palace's institutional-modern decor, combined with the young workers, gives the place the atmosphere of an Indian McDonald's.

"The whole purpose of these places is to provide jobs," says Monica Raphael, the Palace's doe-eyed, twenty-two-year-old manager and daughter of tribal chairman Joseph Raphael. "We employ fifteen teenagers. Native American preference. We try to create a helping atmosphere, try to be as polite as possible." The Bingo Palace and casino combined employ about thirty-five people.

Greg Bailey, casino manager and a long-standing tribal council member, is also there this afternoon. He addresses the issue of the casino's legality. "The U.S. Attorney's office has filed suit against all the gaming tribes in Michigan," he says. "The U.S. is opposed to casinos in states where the casinos are illegal. Our argument is that the State of Michigan licenses Millionaires' Night for the Elks, so they could do the same for the tribes."

Bailey is a man of medium height and build and appears to be somewhere in his late twenties. He wears the expression of a scientist explaining quantum physics to someone hearing about it for the first time—polite, patient, but basically not expecting to be understood. Undoubtedly he is aware that for the uninitiated, Indian tribes have a confusing legal status. They are sovereign nations, but are nonetheless under the jurisdiction of the federal government. In addition, state law sometimes indirectly impacts the tribes in varied ways, as in the case of casino gambling or fishing rights. Over the years this three-way bind has created seemingly endless litigation over matters such as fishing and land rights, taxation, and the routine adoption practice of placing Indian children in non-Indian families (now not allowed). The cases usually have been infinitely long and complex.

A few days later I run into Mike Petoskey, a mild-mannered Ottawa attorney, on the street in Traverse City. I ask him what he thinks of the charge that Indians are being led astray by the gambling—or that they are leading others astray. "I have a hard time with people who sit in judgment," he says, rubbing his eyes—whether from the question or the bright sunlight, I can't tell. "The state has a multimillion-dollar lottery. I just don't know how you'd address that."

A couple of weeks after I visit the Bingo Palace, I'm sitting in the outer reception area of the tribal offices of the Grand Traverse Band, waiting to see tribal chairman Joseph "Buddy" Raphael, when he finally bursts through the front door—a trim, fiftyish man who looks like an older baseball player. "We have fifteen minutes," he says. Raphael has been chairman of this struggling tribe since 1980, when it first achieved federal recognition. To his knowledge, this is the only state in which Indian tribes have moved into casino gambling.

"If allowed to continue, we could become less dependent on federal dollars," Raphael says, looking at his watch. "We run a clean operation. It's a cash business. You have to have strict accountability. We've offered to open up our books to the courts. The Mafia can't come in here. Entry into any controlling aspect of this business is Indian.

"People have a common misconception about gambling— you open the doors, the money flows in. People wouldn't gamble if they couldn't win. Sometimes we lose money. This is not an easy business to be in."

The night I visit the Leelanau Sands Casino is a wet Wednesday in March. I drive through an empty Leelanau County—past sap buckets hanging on trees, past wet trees that look like black cellophane—thinking no one will be at the casino. As I reach the parking lot at the top of the hill, I am amazed to find thirty cars. For a Wednesday night at 6:30, the place is packed.

I don't know what to do in a casino, so I stand at the bar and listen to the barmaid and the bartender talk about their children's report cards. Almost all the people who work here are

Indian, except the barmaid. Almost all the gamblers are white males.

Finally I get up the nerve to move to a blackjack table where no one is and ask the dealer to teach me how to play. "Dewey" is the dealer's name. Behind him are two or three Indian men who seem to be in charge. Occasionally one of them will say peremptorily, "Changing—one hundred dollars." These men are polite but fairly unsmiling, their faces wearing the classic Indian look—and perhaps the gambler's look—of no expression at all.

Reflecting on my conversations with Bailey and Raphael, it occurs to me that the Indians are in a centuries-long game of chance with the government, sometimes winning, sometimes losing, and mostly just trying to stay in the game.

Dewey, the dealer, shows me how to place a two-dollar bet, and I promptly lose two dollars without understanding how or why. He tells me an ace can be counted either as one or eleven, and I think we are both relieved when a real gambler comes and sits down at our table.

This man is my idea of a high roller. Almost immediately, he loses—first sixty dollars, then a hundred dollars—at black-jack. Three more men come and sit at our table. They begin to bet and lose too. Earlier in the week I called the friend of a friend, who's a banker and who won five hundred dollars here, so I know people win, but that night everyone around me loses.

An article on compulsive gambling in the December 1985 issue of *Psychology Today* said that since 1975 the number of people in the United States who gamble has increased from one million to ten million, but frankly, I find gambling boring. Almost certainly, it's because I don't understand the game, but as I sit there, I understand also that gambling is part of life. We all take risks every day; gambling is just the formal expression of this. At any rate, I have sat here long enough—protocol demands that I either place a bet or leave.

Outside in the parking lot, the wet cars gleam in the light from the street lamps overhead. As I go to get in my car I am stopped for a minute by a loud, booming sound, like a jet breaking the sound barrier or distant thunder. For a moment I can't imagine what the sound might be; then I realize it is the sound of the ice breaking up on Grand Traverse Bay. I have never heard this sound before, but a friend told me once that it was a primal sound, like the sound of geese going south in the fall, a sound that one recognizes even if one has never heard it before. Gambling is like that sound, I decide, as I get into the car: less mysterious than I had imagined, more basic and recognizable.

Contemplating the
Shadows of Sturgeon

Rimwalking

MY FRIENDS Jennifer and Scott live in a house that was in a novel; and their neighbor, who never actually lived in their house at all, *did* live in their house in the novel. I visit this house regularly and have been intrigued each time I visit by the line between fiction and nonfiction, the reality we find and the reality we create.

Take my friends' house, for instance, which appeared briefly on the pages of the 1965 bestseller, *What I'm Going to Do, I Think,* by Larry Woiwode (pronounced Why-wood-ee).

"The place in the novel is called the Clausen Place, which is this place," Jennifer says, "and when they walk to it in the novel it's this distance from the cabin Woiwode lived in. But the people he describes and the house he describes are at the Garthe Farm, which is just behind the cabin he lived in when he was writing the novel."

She says the real place that Larry Woiwode lived in was up on the Michigan Bluffs about two miles up the road from the Clausen farm. Jim Garthe is still there, she says, or he's in the long-term-care facility up in the hospital in Northport.

I like to sit in this house and imagine the layers of lives here—old man Clausen bringing windows on his back the three miles from Northport in the early 1900s; Larry Woiwode and his young wife walking here in 1964 from their cabin on the bluffs to a homestead that at that time was abandoned, maybe picking some of the lilacs that bloom so profusely around this house in the spring. I like to imagine Jennifer and Scott imagining Larry Woiwode imagining the lives here.

Jennifer and Scott are sorting and arranging about two thousand books on the makeshift, brick-and-board shelves they've put up in this leaning, crooked, charming 1890s homestead, more books than this house has probably ever seen before.

In the spring the house sits in a nest of cobalt blue lilacs that seem to "glow" blue, taking light from the air and giving back something almost phosphorescent. The memory of that blue light is strong enough to make its presence felt even in winter.

Jennifer is a professor on sabbatical, trying her hand at carpentry and fiction writing. Scott, who has an engineering degree from the University of Michigan, is supporting them with a chimney-cleaning business.

They are new to the Leelanau Peninsula, in love with it, and busy learning its demography, its mythology, its history. They have recently learned an American Indian dawn ceremony, and every day for the last few weeks they have been getting up in the cold dark to go stand on a hill and wait for the moment of first light. They call it rimwalking.

I find rimwalking more interesting than Woiwode's 1960s novel about an angry young man who drinks too much, but the conversation returns to him. "He drank at HOTEL LIQUORS," Jennifer says, referring to a bar in Northport called Woody's. "If you look at the side of the building at Woody's, you can see the faded letters that say HOTEL LIQUORS, so that's why we always call it HOTEL LIQUORS."

They have walked from their house, the Clausen Place, to the Garthe Farm, making the same trip Woiwode did. They have found the same people he found, some of them, and talked to them, creating their own art form, a Mobius strip linking life and art inseparably.

Writers do bring a certain "awareness" to the places they inhabit. When I was in my twenties in Manhattan, thinking about getting divorced and coming back home to the Leelanau Peninsula, a friend said to me, "There are writers there now. Jim Harrison. Tom McGuane."

As it turns out, Tom McGuane was never here, and Jim Harrison was as inaccessible to sightseers then as he is now. But I could come home then. Somehow the place wasn't as isolated, as desolate, knowing that "there are writers there now."

Being comforted by knowing there are writers around has nothing to do with any fatuousness about writers. As *Prairie Home Companion*'s Garrison Keillor said once about himself, "There is no difference between a fat boy lounging on the steps and a man at his typewriter turning out horseshit."

I think wanting to be in a place where there are writers has more to do with what Marshall McLuhan described as the power of writers "to see environments as they really are." A room with a writer in it is more seen, more heard, and a county with a writer in it is too.

Writers often notice things others would prefer to ignore. Annie Dillard, in an essay entitled "Can Fiction Interpret the World?" exhorts writers to be more like schizophrenics and prophets, and to "interpret the raw data of the universe directly." Then she asks the age-old question: "Do artists discover order, or do they make it up?"

This was a question I asked myself as I left Jim Garthe's room in the long-term-care facility at the hospital in Northport. He was not too interested in Woiwode. "QUITE A CHARACTER," he said in the loud voice of the hard of hearing, "TOO MUCH LIQUOR." Then he said, "THEY'VE GOT SOME NICE PICTURES IN THIS BOOK," and pushed a two-foot square Bible across his bed toward me, pointing to a picture of Christ on the cross that looked like something by Hieronymus Bosch. He asked me what religion I was, and I said I was a lapsed Catholic, which wasn't true, but it was all I could think of to say. He said I could come to the Lutheran church in Northport, and if I felt uncomfortable I could sit in the balcony. After this visit I tried to go to HOTEL LIQUORS, but it was closed for the winter.

I spent the next day at the library in Leland, listening to the heating system clack on and off, poring over the works of other Leelanau County writers, going all the way back to Elizabeth Howard Mizner (b. 1907) and up through Jim Harrison (b. 1937).

Leelanau County has had its share of writers. Kurt Luedtke, who wrote the screenplay for *Out of Africa,* wrote it here. Richard Bach of *Jonathan Livingston Seagull* fame used to visit his estranged wife here at Port Oneida, although his seagull was not a Port Oneida seagull.

Barbara Byfield has written a score of books—cookbooks, children's books, mysteries—while commuting between here and Manhattan, but the books have not been about the Leelanau Peninsula. She summered here as a child and played with local children. "I remember," she says, "we had *lessons,* they had *chores.*" But there has been no book yet about this, or about the place.

A 1975 Broadway play, *The Runner Stumbles* by Milan Stitt, was written about an early 1900s murder of a nun by a priest at Holy Rosary in Isadore in the center of the county. Milan Stitt apparently met a girl who had lived here, and she told him about the bizarre and gruesome tale of a nun found under the church, dead, and a priest who'd disappeared. And he wrote about it.

Poet Dan Gerber, of Gerber baby food fame and fortune, who summered here as a child and still visits, has written poems and short stories that could have taken place in Leelanau County. Is this the Leelanau Peninsula Gerber's describing? ". . . A man has a chance here to become . . . one of the elements . . . a migration of time." It feels like the Leelanau, but he doesn't say.

Elizabeth Howard Mizner began writing about the Leelanau Peninsula when she started visiting here in the summer from the University of Michigan, in the years before the Depression. She said that in the 1920s the big activity in Traverse City in the evening after supper was to go and watch the train come in. She wrote romance novels for young girls. Mizner said they used to take the narrow unpaved road that ran along the Bay through the trees out from Traverse City and drive to Lake Michigan near Pyramid Point.

"Calista had loved this north country from the moment when she had first seen it," Mizner writes in *Girl of the North Country*. "With a soft, lulling sound the waves on Lake Michigan washed gently in over the rim of yellow sand, and far out in the wide blue lake lay the Manitou Islands. Calista stood breathless in wonder and joy. It was more, so much more than she had dared to dream."

I'm startled from my reading by someone having a sneezing fit: a gaunt old man in army green jodhpurs is sneezing by the magazine rack. So I don't appear to be staring, I quickly look past him to the Leland River where even the ducks look cold.

Elizabeth Mizner could thrill to the idea of the Grand Traverse Bay region as a frontier, but that's hardly possible for a writer today. Woiwode's angry young man was just right for the Vietnam era, but we've moved on to other issues now. Writers in the last two decades have had a hard job writing anything of permanence because the culture keeps changing so fast that people constantly need new interpretations, new information, new books. "It's no accident that "coping" books have taken over the market. Things have changed so much since Mizner took the two-track out from Traverse City, it's hard to keep up.

On the book jacket of *The Runner Stumbles,* Clive Barnes, a reviewer for the *New York Times,* raves, "An absolutely fascinating play. It is very moving, and it does say something—through the transference via the structural rigors of Roman Catholicism—about the relationship of a man with a woman. It got to me and I cried." I read it that day in the dusty library and I didn't cry.

Maybe in 1975 people could still feel deeply tormented about Catholicism and celibacy, but today these do not seem like burning issues. This isn't because we're smarter than Clive Barnes, but because the intellectual climate of the country has evolved beyond those earlier issues, precisely because its evolved *out of* them.

For the past twenty-plus years of his residence on the Leelanau Peninsula, writer Jim Harrison has eloquently described what surely must be our weather, our landscapes, our bars, the "feel of it" here. His novel *Farmer* and the poems *Letters to Yesenin* come immediately to mind as books that evoke Leelanau County, but only in one novel that I'm aware of, *Warlock,* published in 1981, does he mention the peninsula by name.

"Warlock drove down to Lake Michigan," Harrison writes, "only a few miles from any farmhouse on the hilly Leelanau Peninsula. It was one of those rare lambent, umbrous mornings when the still warm air was full of green haze, and presented the illusion that one lived in a fairy tale."

I recognize that green haze, that umbrous morning, as descriptive of the place I live, but the county is only the backdrop for the book, not its reason for being; the book is replete with references to the ERA, woodstoves, *Penthouse* magazine, *Kojak,* fancy wines, and fancy ways of cooking duck, references that put this book squarely on track with the trends of the early eighties, or before.

Jim Harrison's poetry is often more successful in transcending the periods it was written in than his novels, partly because poetry, like dreams, deals in universal images, and partly because his poetry is often about nature, which so far is the same as it's always been. So when he writes, in *Plain Song,* "The first thunderstorm of March came last night and when I awoke the snow had passed away, the brown grass lay matted and pubic," we know exactly what that March morning is like, and until a Michigan March becomes fundamentally different, we always will.

Religious historian Joseph Campbell said that myth is the edge—old myths and the new ones we are making. "It is the interface," he said, "between what is known and what can't be known, the mystery of life." Poetry inhabits that edge, as do novels when they're first conceived and written, but novels sometimes seem to lose their power sooner than poetry because by their very nature they are trying to define and explain something, to demystify.

In an essay entitled "At the Edge of History," contemporary philosopher William Irwin Thompson has written, "The relation between the event and the larger process is called 'the imagination.' That's the role of the artist. The imagination is where the individual's physical perceptions relate to the perception of his moment in time, his moment in civilization."

And it is this relationship between the imaginer and his civilization that I find so intriguing, which is maybe why I find Jennifer and Scott's rimwalking more interesting than anything in the library; it seems more like the last tree ring, or maybe the most recent one.

Love of place, ancient indigenous rituals, a longing for connection to the land—these are some of the emerging themes at the end of the eighties. Joseph Eps Brown, in an address at the American Museum of Natural History a couple of years ago, said, "In the sixties, in our restlessness with where we found ourselves, we began to turn to the religions and methods of the Orient. But by the seventies, there developed an increasing awareness of spiritual traditions of the Native Americans here, where the sacred values so many of us were seeking were actually rooted in this land."

And so one day recently during a hot and sunny midwinter thaw I visited Scott and Jennifer to see how they were coming with their 5:00 A.M. dawn ceremony, half expecting to discover that they were "lapsed" rimwalkers by this time.

It was a beautiful day for a drive up Eagle Highway, a day that was "lambent and umbrous" and "more than Calista ever dreamed of, much more." This was particularly so since Jennifer was trying to consider how to respond to an attractive invitation to apply for a teaching position at a prestigious eastern university.

"I'm agonizing," she says when I get there, "because I have never in my life felt so connected to a place as I do here. This morning when we went out to our hill, it was incredible. There was a full moon at our back and a magnificent sunrise over the bay. We've discovered some interesting things about the sunrise. I always thought the sunrise was the moment the sun came over the horizon, but there's a moment before that when you're sitting there and your mind is wandering around, when all of a sudden there's this wave or wash of light, like a wave or wash of water, and all of a sudden it's as if your mind fills the sky." She pauses. "This land here, this peninsula, has provided a way into another part of consciousness, a door, and I don't want to leave it."

"Lately it seems people have forgotten their place in the universe," Scott says, "but now I think that's changing. I feel we're connecting more to the land and more to people who've come before us, and will come after us."

And so that's how rimwalking and tree rings and writers all came together in my mind. Undoubtedly by the time this is published, rimwalking itself will be as dated as the wood stove fad. This year's revelation will be next year's embarrassment. Count on it. But whether it is or not, whether Jennifer and Scott stay or go, whether they continue to greet the dawn or don't, rimwalking itself is almost a metaphor for what writers do. Writers advance through the mist to the edge of whatever it is, and the rest of humanity comes clattering up behind them; then the writers move on.

The Land in the Dunes

TAWNY, BURNISHED, CURVACEOUS, the Sleeping Bear Dunes lie like some magnificently indolent female spirit on the northeastern shores of Lake Michigan. Sand, miles of it, with a hem of woodlands around its base and a haze of dune grass over its windblown heights, stretches between two tiny Michigan coastal villages, Empire in the south and Glen Arbor in the north.

Glaciers deposited the sand here more than ten thousand years ago, and the prevailing westerly winds continue to do the rest, blowing some sand from the shore, and blowing more of it from the upper portion of the glacial bluff onto the plateau surface that laymen call dunes. Beneath the sand are ancient glacial moraines, a vast layer cake of sand and gravel. Most of the top covering of sand is a rose-colored quartz, worn smooth by abrasion against sand and rock and as it constantly blows, it moves the dunes by small increments slowly northeastward.

The dunes are desert-like, and yet they aren't; in a desert you can see nothing but sand for miles, and this is true of only a few places in the dunes. Also, in the desert there is low precipitation, while Michigan dunes receive considerable rain. The dunes are more like a mesa of sand, a high plateau from which most of the surrounding countryside is visible. To the east are the small farms and cottages around Glen Lake, to the south is Empire, to the north and west are the Manitou Islands and the blue expanse of Lake Michigan. From many places in the dunes you can see Lake Michigan, and from everywhere you can feel the presence of that big body of water and smell it on the wind.

There is a sense in the dunes of the glaciers having just been there, or being about to come again. Part of this is that six months out of the year you don't have to conjure ice and snow—it's there, and even when it melts in April it feels like it's still there.

In the winter, if Sleeping Bear Bay freezes over, you can walk to the Manitou Islands, a distance of about ten miles. It doesn't take much to imagine that the Manitou Islands were once part of the mainland.

In my dreams at night, as a child growing up on Sleeping Bear Bay, I would sometimes take dreamscape stepping-stones to the islands, as if the glaciers had receded to the point they had nine thousand years ago. Other times, more recently, in dreams perhaps influenced by newspaper articles about holes in the ozone and the global warming trend, I have seen the waters of Lake Michigan rise as high as my mother's hill and have seen Big Glen become again the bay of Lake Michigan it was one hundred fifteen centuries ago.

Only six thousand years ago in this area, in what is called the Nipissing period, an amazing thing happened. The earth's crust, rebounding from the weight of the glaciers, shifted in such a way that the waters that had been flowing north began flowing south. This resulted in a change in the isostasy, or in the equilibrium of the earth's crust. It was phenomenon like this perhaps that made Einstein believe in God. "Religious feeling takes the form of a rapturous amazement at the harmony of natural law," he said in a 1934 speech reprinted in Crown Publisher's *Einstein: Ideas and Opinions.*

The Pleistocene Ice Age lasted two to three million years, until about ten thousand years ago, according to the Encyclopedia Brittanica. Before that the Great Lakes were broad, low river valleys. They were enlarged by the glaciers repeatedly, until they became the lakes they are today.

To get an idea of the time frame for these events, the Pleistocene is after dinosaurs, but before McDonald's and Burger

King. People were around in the Pleistocene but still living in caves and chasing mastodons. Civilization as we know it—toilets, telephones, and self-help groups—is very, very recent. Civilization of any kind is fairly recent—at least on the geologic time scale that deals in millions of years, starting with the 4.6-billion-year-old earth itself—and begins roughly ten thousand years ago with the start of agriculture. William A. Lovis, an archaeologist who prepared a 1984 archaeological report on the Sleeping Bear Dunes National Lakeshore, dates human habitation of the western hemisphere to about forty thousand years ago, with people coming over on the land bridge from Siberia, and prehistoric settlements in Michigan occurring about thirteen thousand years ago. The glaciers advanced and retreated over a long span of time, and it's reasonable to believe that nomadic tribes moved in and out of the area along with them.

When my family moved to the Glen Arbor area in the 1950s, it seemed like there was hardly anyone around. The population of the entire county was 8,647. You could roller skate between towns. The birch trees behind our house were girdled to the height of a human from when the local Ottawa and Chippewa Indians had gathered birchbark for baskets, as recently as the 1930s judging from the age of the trees.

White settlers had first begun moving into the area in the mid-1850s; not too many of those had wanted to stay and farm the sandy soil of the Leelanau Peninsula. Even where there weren't massive dunes, the soil just beneath the surface was the sand and gravel of the glacial moraines.

Henry Schoolcraft explored the Michigan coast from Chicago to Mackinac in 1820. He wrote that the whole Michigan coast was desolate-looking, and the area along the Sleeping Bear Dunes especially so. After waiting out a rainstorm at Manistee on September 6, he and his guides took off again, heading north toward what are now Frankfort, Empire, and Glen Arbor.

"There is great uniformity in the appearance of the coast," he reports in his *Narrative Journal of Travels,* edited by Mentor L. Williams, "which is characterized by sand banks, and pines. In some instances, a stratum of loam is seen beneath the sand,

and the beech and maple are occasionally intermixed with the predominant pines of the forest; but our impression in passing along the coast are only those produced by barren scenery or uncultivated woods." And then he writes, in a little poem presumably of his own making:

No hamlet smoking through the mists of dawn,
No garden blushing with its fostering dew,
No herds wild browsing on the daisied lawn—
No busy village charms the admiring view.

This is the poem of a man who's sat on the bottom of a canoe too long and waited out rainstorms too often, a man who would have probably given a great deal for a hot cup of tea in a house in a hamlet.

At Sleeping Bear, already named that by the Indians, he describes ". . . a bank of sand, probably two hundred feet high, and extending eight or nine miles, without any vegetation, except a small hillock, about the centre, which is covered with pines and poplars, and has served to give name to the place, from a rude resemblance it has, when viewed at a distance, to a couchant bear. There are two islands off this part of the coast which are called the Sleeping Bear Islands." He is referring to the islands today known as South Manitou and North Manitou. The bank of sand he saw from his canoe is actually about four hundred fifty feet high and must have been approximately that when he saw it one hundred thirty years ago. The Sleeping Bear Dunes proper are about four miles long and one mile wide.

Schoolcraft would probably be astonished to learn that the bleak stretch of shoreline he observed in 1820 is now part of a seventy-one thousand acre Sleeping Bear Dunes National Lakeshore with over a million tourists visiting it each year. Much of the coast that looked like wilderness or wasteland to him in 1820 is now covered with condominiums. Ironically, an act of Congress in 1970 preserved the very stretch of shoreline that Schoolcraft found so uninviting.

When I was a young girl in the 1960s, the dunes were where

we would come on prom nights and on dates in the summer. We would sit on the front slope at the Dune Climb and watch the moon over Glen Lake. Sometimes we'd watch the northern lights over Sleeping Bear Bay; the night sky took over at the top of the dunes in the summer, providing a natural spectacle that sometimes included the northern lights, or aurora borealis, over Lake Michigan. The dunes remain a vast outdoor observatory from which people can look at the stars. The dunes were other-worldly at night; once when I was living at the base of the dunes in 1975, scientists from the National Aeronautics and Space Administration came and conducted secret moon-landing experiments in the dunes at night, giving official confirmation to my sense of this otherworldliness.

It is still possible to go up into the dunes at night and observe the stars from there or view the surreal night landscape. The drive through the dunes closes at sunset, but the Dune Climb on M-109 is open twenty-four hours a day. For those physically able to climb the face of the dunes, the dunes at night still offer a rare magic.

It is easy for people to get lost in the dunes and, although this is exceedingly rare, it is possible to get caught in an avalanche there. It has happened at least twice, once in December 1924 when a young man died in one, and once again in February 1980 when a schoolboy was buried in an avalanche but successfully rescued. One theory about the avalanches is that blowing sand builds up over snow, creating air pockets that then give way under human weight. Another theory is that the steep slope of the various dunes, combined with alternating layers of sand and snow, creates layers of differing strengths, which in turn leads to avalanches.

One day in the dry, early spring of 1989, I visited the Sleeping Bear Dunes, taking my eight-year-old and her friend along the Lake Michigan ridge. We drove on the new, wide asphalt road the National Park Service has built across the top of the dunes. When I lived in Manhattan in the 1970s, I used to have a recurrent nightmare that there was a big highway across the top of the dunes and at the topmost point, a Holiday Inn. Now, except for the Holiday Inn, that prescient dream has materialized.

Along the western horizon on the day we visit are clouds that look like enormous tire tracks, voluminous tire track clouds. It is a cold, sunlit day. The air has a fruit-like smell, like apples. All along the ground small tufts of beach grass have those small, delicate circles around them, the strands of grass— perfect compasses, making perfect little geometric "pi" signs all over the dunes.

The sun is bright, flashing, like flashing mirrors. Here and there in the brown woods behind us are patches of snow. On top of the dunes the wind is blowing so loud you can hear it. I think the wind is always blowing on top of the dunes—at least on the lake side. Once when I was young and in my teens and didn't know any better, I spent a night on the west bluff of the dunes. What I remember about that night is the way the wind blew unceasingly, like white noise; it just never shut off. It seemed to die down about sunrise, and I must have fallen asleep then. I awoke about 9:00 A.M., hot and sweaty and dazed in full sun.

The girls and I get out at the deck built over the west bluff face. This is where I used to watch sturgeon in the shallows below. Big and black and the size of humans, they looked like divers in wet suits. Sturgeon are an ancient species dating back three hundred seventy-five million years, to the Middle Devonian. The ones in the Great Lakes, now almost extinct, used to be so plentiful along this stretch of coast that they were considered a nuisance fish because they tore up fishermen's nets. In the 1800s they were speared and killed by the hundreds as they came in to spawn, and then they were stacked and burned like cordwood.

My daughter finds a Petoskey stone, a remnant from the days when Michigan was a saltwater sea, when Michigan wasn't Michigan but just a nameless place maybe somewhere down near where Brazil is now, when the continents were all askew from what they are today. I get vertigo thinking about it, and vertigo staring down at the Lake Michigan shore four hundred fifty feet below.

We walk back to the car. I picture Michigan as it appears in one of those infrared photos taken from outer space. Michigan, like a mitt on the face of the globe, melting back down toward Florida and the Silurian. Michigan, a geographic anomaly, a peninsula in the center of a continent, surrounded by water, but not by oceans.

"How did the dunes get here?" my daughter wants to know. Isostasy, I tell her. Glaciers. Ice sheets several thousand feet thick. They came and went. Glaciers. Wind. Thousands of years. The wind blew the sand into dunes. It took a long time. But she can't take it in—the time spans are just too vast, the concepts too abstract.

As I tell her this, I'm reminded of the Bronx truck driver who drove the moving van filled with my Manhattan belongings to the farmhouse at the base of the dunes. He arrived on a bitter January day, so bitter he felt compelled to give me three of those big moving truck quilts they wrap around furniture—one for me and each of my children, I think now in retrospect. He was a big man, big-hearted, thick Bronx accent, a city man. "How did they get all that sand there?" he asked sociably. I looked at him, totally nonplussed for a moment, and then said, "Big trucks."

The more I tried to explain to my daughter that day how the sand got there, the more I longed for a simple explanation, like the one I gave the moving man. Big trucks, perhaps the kind of trucks that had made the tire tracks in the sky, celestial trucks. Fortunately with children you never have to stay on one subject too long, and we moved quickly on to lunch, something we could all understand.

Reflections on Our Connections to the Land

OUTSIDE MY WINDOW the mist is rising from the pond. A moment ago when I stuck my head out the door I could hear the creek rattling across the frozen ground with a sound like one of those Jamaican barrel drums I used to hear on the streets of New York. There is a mood in the weather and in me that I recognize as the season of reflection. This is the time of year up north when the days are short and dark and one's mind turns naturally to the larger questions, such as what are we doing here and does democracy work and what will this place look like in twenty years?

It was a strange summer; strange fall, too. Daily, people called to tell me about one more assault on the land. The state highway department cut large maple trees along M-72. Traverse City wanted to sell parkland on the bay to a mall developer. The Homestead condominium resort in Glen Arbor wanted to put a golf course along the wetlands of the Crystal River. The federal government put a giant road through the woods in the national lakeshore when a little road would have been better.

But I cannot complain about "those developers." My own father was a developer. I can remember when he came here and bought up the whole side of a lake. There were no cottages there then. There was nothing. I can recall how hot the day was and how my four sisters and I all went swimming in our underwear. There was nobody around. I remember how quiet it was.

Now there are a lot of cottages there, and the people in those cottages—some of them—are complaining about the golf course that The Homestead wants to put in along the Crystal River wetlands. I am with them. I would rather have the swamp than the golf course, but at the same time I recognize that the land where their cottages are would look better if their cottages weren't there. And I am also aware that even if it isn't absolutely true that five girls wouldn't have gone to college if their father hadn't been a developer, there is an inescapable connection between the money my father made off the land and the advantages my sisters and I have enjoyed.

Most of my friends are environmentalists; most of their parents were not. We sit in each others' living rooms and talk about this. My friend Stephanie's father is a mining consultant; her grandfather was a mining engineer and got malaria in the rain forests in South America before anybody thought there was anything worth saving in a rain forest. In one or two generations we've gone from beating back the wilderness to trying to save it. "A little wetlands here and there is not trivial," Stephanie says, "because it's happening around the globe. Destroying ecosystems is like randomly removing the rivets in an airplane; you don't know how many rivets you have to remove before the wing falls off."

The Grand Traverse region is no newcomer to development. From the first wave of settlers in the 1850s to the first development boom in the 1970s, the area has brought a gleam to the eye of many an entrepreneur. But there's something different going on now. Fifteen years ago the environmental issues were fought on a community by community basis. Now there's a broad base of support for environmental issues that extends beyond the immediate neighborhoods in question. The developers are more sophisticated this time around and give lip service to environmental concerns—the proposed Homestead golf course, for instance, is frequently described as "an environmentally sensitive golf course." And the environmentalists are more streetwise and use the Freedom of Information Act, court injunctions, and public protest to stop the projects they see as detrimental.

Sometimes when I go to these environmental issue meetings, I feel sorry for the developers because not only are all my friends and half my neighbors allied against them, but I see in them my father, or my father's generation. Bob Kuras, the owner-developer of The Homestead, even sort of looks like my father: the same bald, high forehead, the same unusual mix of wanting to make money and having a finely tuned sensitivity to the qualities of the land. It seems unfair to castigate the developers for doing what this society has always valued and rewarded: making money by developing the frontier. And in some ways northern Michigan is still a frontier, or is seen as such by entrepreneurs. And the positivism of the developers, the can-do mentality, the lack of self-awareness are not without their charms.

Yet we are talking here about a part of the country that is not only desirable for development—the high hills and deep bays of the glacier-carved northern Lake Michigan shoreline—but an area to which people are moving for quality of life reasons, for that connection to the land. People have given up, in some cases, money and power to be in this environment, and they are not willing to see someone else achieve money and power by exploiting it.

In my friend Jennifer's house at the tip of the Leelanau Peninsula, near Northport, I sit and we talk about this. Jennifer is a professor of communications who is taking a break from teaching to do some writing. She now works part-time as a carpenter, and continues to review manuscripts to support herself while she writes. Stacks of manuscripts—hers and other people's—sit on her coffee table, while on the clothesline above us hang the drying long johns she wears as a carpenter.

"These are not sterile, dry public planning issues," she says of the crowded town-hall meetings. "They're issues that make a difference in what we see when we walk out our front doors. We're here because we have this relationship to the land. I can't go a day without knowing the phase of the moon and what flowers are in bloom, because they impose themselves on us."

Jennifer's father was a lumber broker, and the two of us know that the issues are broader and deeper than just "those developers" and "those environmentalists." The issues go back to the way this country was founded, to the view of the land as an essential part of democracy and free enterprise. The phrase "life, liberty and the pursuit of happiness" was originally John Locke's "life, liberty and the right to own property."

Our ideas of democracy are inextricably tied up with land acquisition and land exploitation. It is a not very pleasant or oft-remarked truth that the coffers of this country were filled time and again with sales of lands we took from the Indians. "When we reached California and our natural borders," as one history book euphemistically summed up this carnage, then we were, within a short time, broke again, and we had to start levying the land taxes that people in my family—at least in the 1600s—left England to escape.

I would like to be able to tell myself that my father was a "good developer" and that nobody in my family ever killed Indians, bootlegged whiskey, or kept slaves. But I know for a fact that one uncle, George Stocking, fought Indians for a living, and I suspect that only the teeniest search would reveal relatives and past activities I'd pay someone dearly to remove from the records. None of us, no matter how recently we arrived here, can escape the history and values that this country has created. That's not all bad, for only by knowing the truth of the past can we see the shape of the future.

What I see happening in Glen Arbor and Traverse City—and the golf course in Glen Arbor and the mall in Traverse City are only two of a dozen environmental issues that have cropped up here in the last year and are happening not just here but all over the country—is that people are finally evolving a set of values and ideas about their relationship to the land. They are fighting for not just their ten acres, but for the integrity of the land base and the quality of life: "what we see when we walk out our doors," as Jennifer said, or "the swamp that can't be replaced," as Stephanie said.

Stephanie has called this "a paradigm shift"; someone else called it "an evolution in consciousness." What I see happening in our relationship to the land is people feeling that it is both wrong and stupid to destroy the land base because the long-term bad effects will far outweigh the short-term "perks." I see a parallel here to what happened in attitudes toward slavery. For hundreds of years people kept slaves; nobody thought too much about it, and there were lots of intellectual arguments supporting the practice. Then about a hundred thirty years ago this country fought a bloody civil war over slavery that effectively ended it. Not too long after that they got rid of the practice of indentured servants, and the 1920s and 1930s saw the formation of labor unions—again, bloody fights—and eventually labor laws. Our consciousness about human labor, if you will, evolved.

The same is now happening in terms of our relationship to the land. The other day I walked to the top of our hill to look at the whitecaps on Lake Michigan. When you can see the whitecaps on Lake Michigan two miles away there's usually a thirty-mile-an-hour wind blowing, and as I was standing there in this gale, I was struck by the power and beauty of the land, the power and beauty of its past, its people and its future. On some level I have faith in them, in us, and I want to see what will happen next. It is more interesting with the people here than without them, and I believe that, no matter how difficult, in the end what will happen will be the right thing for both the people and the land. It is interesting to watch people make the shift from physically defending their land to defending the integrity of the land base, whether it is theirs or not, and I'm not about to turn in my front row ticket to this event.

Listening for the First
Smelt Run

WHAT SIXTH SENSE lets fish know when it's time to spawn?
This is the thought that crosses my mind as I think I hear the
first faint sounds that tell me the smelt might be running.

Not that I can actually "hear" the fish, for I imagine they are
fairly soundless in their swimming, but I can hear the seagulls
circling over Houdek's Creek, hear those cat-cry, lady-love-
making, seagull mewling noises carried on the wind up Lake
Leelanau to my house.

It is always a warm day when the smelt run. The kind of early
spring day when you hang your wash on the line for the first
time. The kind of day when there's not only that seagull sound
on the wind, but a scent, a slightly sweet smell, of sap, of
pungent old leaves, of woods relieved of a winter's worth of
snow, a tantalizing scent that calls you outside to simply sniff it.

To get a feeling for the kind of day I mean, first try to picture
the Leelanau Peninsula, a narrow wedge of land jutting out into
Lake Michigan two hundred eighty miles north of Chicago.
Picture that peninsula's middle, where I live; then picture
Houdek's Creek inlet, about three miles northwest of my place
on inland Lake Leelanau. Then imagine a high wind, about tree
level, carrying that sound.

Last year when I heard the sound of the seagulls carried on
the wind up the lake, I didn't know what it was. I got on my

bike and followed the sound around to the other side of the lake where all the seagulls were congregated over Houdek's Creek inlet. The banks of Lake Leelanau are high and rocky here, more like places along Lake Michigan than an inland lake, and white gravel and sand lead steeply to a narrow shore. On this particular day the wind was whipping across from the west, almost visible. Whitecaps the size of chickens were scudding across Lake Leelanau's icy, blue-green waters. The seagulls were as thick as the whitecaps, only slightly smaller and in the air.

A boy was coming along the road, a boy with a baseball cap pulled down level with his eyes. Surely, I thought to myself, a boy like this would know why the seagulls were circling over Houdek's Creek inlet.

As soon as the question was out of my mouth, I'd guessed the answer. The boy apparently thought the question was so dumb it wasn't worth raising his baseball cap visor to look at me. "Because the smelt are running?" I asked. The wind blew the words back at me.

"Yeah," he said then, raising his eyes just enough so he could see me but I still couldn't see him, "but probably not 'til tonight."

I knew enough not to ask how the seagulls knew the smelt were running, before they ran. I knew enough not to ask why smelt ran at night, or if the sound of the seagulls had brought him, too, to check out Houdek's Creek.

I rode home with the wind at my back. Vaguely I recalled hearing that smelt spawned in three-year cycles, swimming the Great Lakes until they returned to the same gravelly creek beds where they'd been spawned. Something about the changing water temperature in the spring or the lengthening daylight brought them back after the ice went out on the big lakes. But from there on, it was anybody's guess. They ran at different creeks at different times, anywhere from late March to early May, depending on something only the smelt knew.

I remembered smelt-dipping as a small child, further south on the peninsula, down near what is now a condominium complex called The Homestead near Glen Arbor but what was then just Art Huey's place. I recalled a night on the Crystal River when the smelt were running by the millions; I stood with skinny ten-year-old's legs in the slippery swarm of fish and dipped with a macaroni strainer. That night when my husband came home from work I told him smelt were running at Houdek's Creek.

My husband and I have returned to the northern Michigan of our childhoods, after nearly thirty years away for him and half that for me. He has come back from Chicago and Indianapolis. I have come back from Ann Arbor and Manhattan. We came back because we missed the seasons, the sense of place, the people. My husband's ancestors, Ottawa Indians, had been from Harbor Springs—further north on Lake Michigan—longer than it had been Harbor Springs. He, too, remembered the annual spring smelt-dipping ritual, with people and fish thick in the cold Lake Michigan inlets.

The smelt run is one of the first signs of spring in the north. People are glad, after a long winter, to have a sign like this. Word of the fish is spread quickly, from grocery store to bar to hardware store to post office to gas station. Did the smelt wonder how we knew? I guess someone who lived close to a creek off Lake Michigan would see a few stragglers come up and then tell everyone.

And so one night, soon after the smelt ran at Houdek's Creek, they ran at Belanger's Creek. My husband went, leaving me and a sleeping baby at 2:00 A.M., to go stand in a cold creek. I didn't know he had gone until about 4:00 A.M. when I awoke to find his side of the bed cold and got up to put wood on the fire.

Belanger's Creek wasn't much, he said when he came home at gray light. A lot of so-called sports fishermen drinking and making the usual remarks about the Indians at Peshawbestown a half mile north. It was dark. He guessed they couldn't see he was Indian. He went on down to Weaver's Creek. "There was no one there but me," he said. "I looked at the lights over at Traverse City at the end of the bay. I wondered how many

years it would be before the lights, I guess I mean the people, would be out as far as Weaver's Creek."

As we cleaned fish I wondered what I was doing taking the lives of little creatures who only hours before had been looking forward to spawning on the clean gravel. I remembered a story my sister had told me about reading a *National Geographic* to a little Inuit boy up at Frobisher Bay in Canada. "Bang," he said, when they got to a picture of a baby seal. My sister had been shocked. First at him, then at herself. Of course, she realized, it was natural for him to see the seal as food and clothing and lamplight. But was it natural for me to be participating in the "death" of these fish? Did I need them? Or was I indulging a romantic fantasy of what I only imagined to be one of the natural rhythms of people on the planet? I was too intellectual, by far, I could see that. "Is this milt or roe?" I asked my husband.

He looked a little piqued. He'd already told me that in his family the women (meaning his mother and four sisters) cleaned the fish, while the men (meaning him and his father) caught them. He'd gotten used to women's lib, but he hadn't bargained for cleaning fish. "I think the yellow is the eggs," he said in the stiff voice he used for hiding his feelings, "and the grayish stuff is the milt. I'm just guessing."

I didn't tell him I had found a recipe in a fancy French cookbook for raw smelt with roe dressing. I felt a little squeamish myself. It seemed to take forever to clean a pail of smelt. I couldn't imagine wanting to cook that many, let alone eat them.

The smelt were little and reminded me of goldfish. As I rolled one first in egg and then in cornmeal and fried it in hot bacon grease, my enthusiasm for smelt-dipping waned. I began to wish each gutted fish was miraculously whole again and swimming in the creek.

Yet I was not ready to let on about my disappointment. "The kitchen is hot and greasy," I said with a wave of my arm at imaginary cooking odors. "Let's eat at the picnic table outside." We ate in the backyard under maple trees that I could imagine, but that were not, in red bud. We wore our down coats, eating the rapidly cooling smelt in blinding spring sunlight. I was aware of eating the same fish I had just cleaned. I wondered if their families were still in the creek. Somehow the whole experience of smelt dipping wasn't the way I'd remembered it. I'd remembered the excitement of the catch, the mounds of hot, delicious smelt my mother had cooked. Was it always on a Sunday? We would eat until noon.

Certainly the smelt had not changed.

Rather it was I who had changed.

I now saw the smelt as nuclear families. I had anthropomorphized the fish in a way that never would have occurred to my child's mind.

As I sat in the cold sunlight it was with a sense of sadness that I realized I had been away too long, a sense of sadness perhaps my husband had felt all along. I had lived in cities too long, been away from fish too long. Perhaps the old instincts will return; the desire to dash down to a cold creek in the middle of the night because the smelt might be running will seep back into my personality in the slow imperceptible way it seeped out. I don't know. What I do know is that on a cold, sunny day in early spring last year I found out that the exploration of atavistic urges sometimes brings us up against the hard wall of our own so-called sophistication so we discover not our "roots," but the experiences that separate us from them.

A Little Farm in the
Leelanau Hills

FOR ANYONE who has ever thought of chucking it all and moving to the country—maybe buying a little farm somewhere where they could grow their own food and live off the income from the extra produce—they might take a lesson from John and Julia Brabenec, who have done it, successfully and happily, but not without a tremendous commitment of time, energy, emotion, and philosophical devotion to rural self-sufficiency.

John and Julia Brabenec are neighbors of mine on the Leelanau Peninsula. A couple in their early sixties, they came to this peninsula fifteen years ago. Originally from Detroit, they left there in 1969 and, after spending a few years in Colorado and Canada, eventually came here where they had honeymooned in 1948.

On their small, hilly farm the Brabenecs grow beautiful organic vegetables and fancy fruits and sell them to local markets. They live simply—without running water or other modern conveniences—and heat with wood.

They are intellectuals who have, among other things, organized a speakers' forum called the Leelanau Concerned Citizens that meets about once a month to discuss social and political issues. Speakers from Amnesty International, South Africa, the Sanctuary movement, and other places have come to Leland to this group, which sometimes meets in the school cafeteria. John said he organized it because he thought it was important to be able to look in the eyes of someone who was telling you something. They are both also accomplished thespians active in local theater.

Even before I knew John and Julia, but had only heard of them, as one inevitably hears about interesting people in a sparsely populated rural community, I had this image of them as being like the man and woman in the "Peace and Plenty" cross-stitch that used to hang in my grandmother's kitchen. It showed a man picking crimson apples from a cross-stitch tree and a hoop-skirted woman gathering golden flowers in a cross-stitch garden.

For many of my friends, especially those who have moved here recently from cities, John and Julia's rural life is an archetype of the kind of rural life they'd like for themselves. "My ideal of the way I'd like to live is John and Julia," a friend raptured to me one day.

Partly because I wanted to get inside that idealized cross-stitch picture and partly because I'd become fascinated with them as a couple after watching them on the stage for two hours as they performed the male and female lead in *Foxfire*, a play about a pioneer couple's journey through their life and marriage, I wanted to get to know them better. And so one day I arranged to visit them.

John and Julia's farm is in an aspen grove in the leeward foothills of the Lake Michigan Bluffs near Northport. It sits at the end of a long two-track on land that used to belong to Julius Patanaquat, an Ottawa Indian. So recently was this peninsula settled—1854 was the year the first white man came ashore here, according to available records—that the presence of the Ottawa Indians who lived here for the previous eons is still very real. John and Julia sometimes find old dishes and tools from the turn of the century that they think were from Mr. Patanaquat's tenure on the land.

They have a small house, a medium-sized shop, and an unfinished larger house they've been building for several years. Gardens as neat as a *New Yorker* cover run along the northern side of the dirt driveway, while off to the west, up past a field, are the apple orchards in rows above Lake Michigan. The graceful gray-barked aspen trees are like big-skirted ladies folk-dancing around the farm.

Julia is a small woman and so young looking that when I see her in the garden I mistake her for her oldest daughter, a dance teacher in Traverse City. John is a tall, spare man with a tan that doesn't make one think of Florida and tanning salons but of outdoors and work.

Their gardens are carefully tended, with a visual perfection you usually see only in gardening catalogues. They use no chemical fertilizers or pesticides on the vegetables. With some of the bugs, such as the tomato hornworms, Julia picks them off by hand. With others they use an organic insecticide called bacillus thuringiensis, a biological control for cabbage worms. They say they farm organically because they are concerned about poisoning the soil and poisoning the population. Julia says that by keeping the soil in top condition and keeping the plants healthy, they can largely avoid a need for insecticides. "It's not as big a problem as you might imagine," John says.

They have seven acres of fruit trees, and on these one commercial pesticide is used. Their fruit varieties are uncommon and flavorful. It was from this farm that I first tasted the Raritan Rose peach—a white-fleshed peach with an aftertaste of raspberries. They also grow several varieties of apples, including a Japanese apple called Mutsu and an apple called SpyGold that is a cross between a Northern Spy and a Golden Delicious and that grows to the size of a grapefruit.

Their house, inside, has a frontier elegance. A dark velvet sofa. White lace antimacassars. A blue enamel kettle is steaming on the stove, and on the kitchen table are little jars of red pepper preserves. Copies of *The Nation, Utne Reader,* and *Country Journal* are on the table beside me. Photos of their three children and several grandchildren line the walls.

"This life is not for everyone," John says. "There are times when I wonder why we're doing it. Even if you change your standard of living, there are still basic expenses. Food. Gas. We don't have running water. Anyone trying this for the first time would miss hot showers every day. It requires a lot of discipline. Every bit as much as living in the city. More so. You have to discipline yourself.

"You don't have to wonder what to do, just what to do next," John says.

"You're either in the garden or the orchard," Julia says.

"I can't wait to get outside in the morning," John says. His voice trails off. He looks off into space for a moment. His voice is gracious, musing, yet intense. He has one of those long, narrow faces, deeply lined and deeply tanned, that makes him look like a thirteenth-century woodcut.

"John was a printer," Julia says. "When he quit printing was when they blackened the windows and he couldn't look outside anymore. We'd always lived in the country outside Detroit and had our own garden but. . . ."

"When they went to computerized printing," John explains, "the computers were light sensitive and they had to cover the windows."

He reflects for a moment. "I sometimes wonder if it was still hot type, if I'd be doing it, but I don't think so. There seems to be something in your being. . . . I remember when I was about ten years old, my parents were thinking about buying a small farm in the country. They never did, but I got real excited about raspberries."

Both John and Julia are of Czech ancestry and from the Detroit area. Julia grew up on a farm near Richmond, and John grew up on Detroit's southwest side. They met at the *Detroit News,* where Julia worked in advertising and John was a printer—like his father and grandfather before him. They were married soon after meeting and recently celebrated their fortieth wedding anniversary.

In this day of skyrocketing divorce rates, the fact that they've been married forty years is as out of the ordinary as the organic gardening they do, maybe more so.

"We have a really strong relationship," John says. "We really love one another and have a lot in common."

"We're evenly matched," Julia says.

One year for their anniversary their three children, Elisa, Jeff, and Rebecca, told them to expect a surprise on their anniversary, July 23, but they didn't know what kind of surprise to expect. On that day they were both working in their garden and a limousine came down the long two-track to their house. The chauffeur told them to get dressed and come with him. They both got dressed up—John never did change out of his work boots—and were taken to a fancy restaurant where their children, who had flown in from all over the country, were waiting for them.

In the dim light of their farm home, as they talk, John and Julia are testy and tender with each other by turns, at once courteous with each other and trying hard to be honest about their feelings. I learn that they yearly cut ten cords of wood with Swedish crosscut saws, and I ask how many more years they think they'll be able to do that. "Not too many," Julia sighs. At almost the same time John says, stretching, "Another thirty years." This kind of byplay between them, some verbal, most not, creates the sense that their life's journey, in terms of exploring and living the values they believe in, is also the journey and exploration of their relationship.

Both say they were influenced in their decision to live a rural, farming life by the example of Helen and Scott Nearing. Scott Nearing, a Wharton professor who was fired from the Wharton School of Economics in the 1920s for his then-radical views against child labor, moved shortly thereafter to the New England wilderness. In the 1920s, New England still had wilderness. The Nearings built their own house out of stone and were well-known lecturers for the causes of vegetarianism, pacifism, and ecology—fifty years ahead of their time. They wrote several books together, the most popular of which was *Living the Good Life—How to Live Sanely and Simply in a Troubled World*. They were cult figures, of a sort, for a more cult-naive generation, and young people of the forties and fifties would trek to the Nearing's New England retreat to sit at the feet of these masters of the good life. Scott Nearing died in 1983—at the age of one hundred.

The Nearings and the Brabenecs carry on a tradition that goes back to the founding of this country. "That individuals could start over again, and if necessary, reinvent themselves," writes historian Frances Fitzgerald, "is one of the great legends of American life." The Quakers, the Mormons, the Transcendentalists—Thoreau at Walden Pond—were all trying to live what we call the considered life. "This country was founded by visionaries," Fitzgerald writes; she quotes John Winthrop's famous remark to his seasick flock as he crossed the Atlantic to found the Massachusetts Bay Colony: "We must consider that we shall be a City Upon a Hill—the eyes of all people shall be upon us."

The desire for freedom and opportunity, to live a vision of a better life, which brings people to America in the first place, seems to keep them moving once they get here, and the seductive beauty of the Leelanau Peninsula has lured more than one couple away from economically secure urban lives.

"You have to be able to accept the hardships nature gives you—dry weather, too much rain. But we have a lot to be thankful for," John says. "We love the land. We live close to nature. We're both in good health. Sometimes I say to myself, 'Do you want to go work in a factory in Flint? Grow up.'"

One of the things the Brabenecs have in common, in addition to the gardening, is a shared commitment to pacifism. They both worked for the nuclear freeze and are proud of the fact that Leelanau County had more signatures for the freeze than any other county in Michigan.

Their pacifism even extends to mice, and Julia tells the story of the time they were live-trapping field mice that kept getting into their house. John rigged up a cistern with a plank and a trip and some peanut butter at the bottom of the deep, smooth-sided pickle crock. But they were catching so many mice—and carting them out to the field daily in an effort to remove them from the house without killing them, that Julia said the mice were beginning to look familiar. One day she took some white-out from her writing desk and painted the mouse's tail. Sure enough, the next day there was the same mouse, white tail and all. "He knew where to get some good peanut butter and a free ride besides," Julia said. John then drove the mouse three miles from their home, and the mouse did not return.

We talk about the play they were in, *Foxfire,* and how their lives in some ways mirror those of Annie and Hector, the characters in the play, and how they mirror, too, the lives of men and women generally. Like Annie and Hector's pioneer life, John and Julia's life is physically hard and would be especially difficult for a woman alone to maintain. Julia says, almost apologetically, looking at John, "I wouldn't leave right away [if something happened to John], but I would leave. It's too hard. I couldn't do it alone."

A few days later, after a play practice in the Suttons Bay Fire Hall, after the final scene in which Hector dies and Annie puts the coins on his eyes and sings, "Today is done, dear Lord. Tomorrow's sun, dear Lord, is sure to come," Julia comes up to me and says, "I want to change what I said before. If something happened to John, I wouldn't leave. I'd stay. But if one of my children needed me, I'd go to them."

The Nearings left Manhattan during the 1930s Depression and went to rural New England to build their version of a city on a hill, an ideal community. They did so in part to escape the economic ravages of the times by being self-sufficient. But the economic collapse of the thirties didn't last, and the Nearings, along with the rest of the country, enjoyed unprecedented prosperity and leisure.

By contrast, John and Julia Brabenec left Detroit in the 1960s, at the peak of one of the most affluent periods in this country's history, a time when people could afford to throw away or give away old furniture, cars, appliances. Gas was about fifty cents a gallon, and food was about half as expensive as it is now. In the intervening years inflation and the oil crisis have changed all that, and the Brabenecs have less leisure time and more work than they'd anticipated.

"When we first came here," Julia says, "it seems I used to have time to go sit on top of the hill, watch the clouds, write a poem; now there's no time for anything but work."

"I'd like to explore this money issue a little more," John says. "I don't know anyone who has enough money. Even if you heat with wood and haul water, you still have to have an automobile. You still have taxes on the land. We get up around 6:00 A.M. and stay up until midnight."

"One time John fell asleep putting on his boots," Julia says. "I found him on the porch."

But both say the closeness to the land and the freedom they have are worth the amount of work it requires. "We want to live simply," John says, "to have low impact on the environment, to leave it the way we found it. I guess I always think of the upland plover in the mists around our fields. They come in the spring and they build their nests. They have a real pretty song as they fly high above the fields. They lay their eggs. They feed their young. And in the fall when they leave, you wouldn't know, from looking where they'd been, that they were here. I guess I'd like to be like that."

The Passage of Time at
The Homestead

THE HOMESTEAD has a history that I love, that tells the history of the Leelanau Peninsula in miniature. Imagine The Homestead first the way it is today: a 500-unit condominium resort on Lake Michigan where the Crystal River comes into Sleeping Bear Bay. It is a chichi and comfortable place with four restaurants, several elegant shops, five clay tennis courts, four pools, a cabana, and several miles of nature trails.

Imagine that you arrive from Detroit on a hot summer night that is merely balmy by the time you reach the Glen Arbor pines. You pull in past the liveried guards at The Homestead gate, up the sweeping driveway and slowly through the trees, down to where the Crystal River runs into the bay.

You step from your car and hear the faint sound of Chopin coming across the parking lot from the bar at the racquet club. The air has the sweet smell of balm of Gilead. You are with a favorite friend. You move down toward the tennis courts and dance the pas de deux before moving inside to the Balcony Bar for a nightcap. You retire to your condominium aerie in Ridge Top, or you find your way down the dunes to the Sandpiper condo, a little place that opens onto the water.

You wake the next morning, find your refrigerator stocked as requested, make a light breakfast of eggs benedict and fresh melon on the sun-dappled deck, and are entertained by a mother deer and a fawn who make their way down to the water on the other side of the river to drink from the bank.

Move back fifty years in time to the thirties—imagine rattan, painted wicker, bouquets of orange lilies in carnival glass. You and your husband have motored up from Grosse Pointe to visit the kids: John Jr. enrolled in Camp Leelanau for the summer, Adelia in Camp Kohana. You and John Sr. will stay at "the Inn"—the big, brown, rambling, splendidly rustic building set against the steep, wooded hill where the Crystal River flows out into Sleeping Bear Bay.

You find yourself humming the tune to "Nothing Could be Finer Than to be in Carolina in the Morning" as you unpack your tennis whites, golfing clothes, sailing shoes. These two weeks in June will be "rustic"—delicious, home-cooked meals at the inn, golf and horseback riding in the D. H. Day Estate, daily swimming and sunbathing at the mouth of the Crystal River, and chinese checkers with the other visitors at the inn when it rains. After that, it's Mackinac Island and the height of the summer social season. But for now, it's time out of time at The Homestead.

Close your eyes and let time collapse around you again; open your eyes to 1854 on the Crystal River. You are a young boy visiting the Indian camp to see if anyone knows where your cows are. The Indians are fishing for sturgeon and whitefish here before moving on to Harbor Springs for the remainder of the summer.

The camp is ideally situated in the clearing by the mouth of the river. Indian children swim in Lake Michigan and play on the shore while their dark-eyed mothers weave marsh grass into mats. The women laugh and talk in light, lilting voices.

Islands the Indians call *man-ee-dow,* or spirit, loom in the bay they call *mishemokwa,* or sleeping bear. Their words for these things hint at ancient myths and give an added mystery to this already mysterious land. A young girl, your age, helps you find your cows and then, giggling, begins to teach you the word for corn—*dominick quashegan*—and kerosene—*washe conge conombo.*

On the way home, over the hill toward your cabin, you see

an enormous black mother bear and her cub a hundred yards ahead on the trail. You wait for them to amble off into the brush before herding your slow, cud-chewing beasts along the way, musing, as you walk, at the vast quantity of game—bear, deer, duck, partridge. The Indians must wonder at the two white families with their chickens and cows dopily slaving away to produce food in a land where it is everywhere available and abundant. Earlier in the spring, there were so many passenger pigeons that their migration darkened the sky; when they came to roost in the fields, they were so tame, they could be caught in two hands.

It is summer, nearly sunset, and yet so far north it will be late evening before the last light fades over the Sleeping Bear Dunes. You go home and fall asleep in ten o'clock twilight, dreaming of a girl teaching you how to say "kerosene" in another language.

The Man Who Had
Wild Chickens

From the road the dark shapes in the bare branches of the trees down by the bay look like they might be pieces of burned newspaper that had blown there from someone's trash barrel. Not until I see a dog chase one of the dark shapes up into a tree do I realize the dark shapes are birds.

It is cold and windy as I walk down the old trail toward Grand Traverse Bay to get a closer look. Not crows. Not seagulls. Chickens, I finally decide, uncharacteristically roosting high in the trees beside this northern bay of Lake Michigan. Nearby, fisherman Art Duhamel's gear is all around, and his fish house with the totem pole outside has smoke coming out of the chimney. But there doesn't seem to be anybody around the place.

I walk back up the road to where my friends are doing some survey work on the Peshawbestown Indian reservation ball diamond. "Art's got chickens," I say. "Weird chickens."

Everyone laughs. *"Wild* chickens," someone corrects, "Art's got *wild* chickens."

The story as it unfolds is that someone someone knew had crossbred a bunch of chickens to produce a breed that could survive on their own in the northern woods. The experiment had succeeded—after a fashion. The wild chickens found their own food and water, eschewed the henhouse for the trees, hid their eggs, were too tough to eat, and couldn't be caught by man or beast. No one would take them but Art Duhamel.

The talk up on the road around the survey transit ranges from how the chickens could survive in the cold, to the best method for cooking a really tough chicken (pressure cooker), to the chickens in laying factories not having enough room to move around, to the hormones and antibiotics fed to today's chickens, to the excessive amounts of yellow fat in the chickens at the supermarket.

We are not farming people any more, so this talk of chickens is a bit giddy and farfetched. Who knows anything about chickens? None of us do. But we like the idea of the wild chickens as a small, symbolic protest on behalf of all the chickens in the laying factories.

Later that week I call Dr. Cal Flegal, the Michigan State University Co-op Extension's poultry man. "Inneresting, inneresting," he says. "I can see if you got some fighting cock and some bantam, so long as they got some food sometimes, they'd survive. I remember reading about a flock of wild chickens on an island off the coast of Australia a few years back, read about it in that *Scientific American*." I ask him about the blue eggs these wild chickens are sometimes said to have laid. "A blue egg means somewhere along the line you got a chicken from South America named Aracauna involved. If you get the right kind of chicken they can go a little wild. We used to have some like that on the farm back home, birds that would move off into the woods. We used to shoot 'em with a twenty-two. If they're in a place without too many predators—foxes, owls, hawks—they could survive like that for a while."

A couple of days later I stop by to see Art Duhamel. Art is an Indian fisherman of considerable reputation. This morning he's sitting in brown snowpants and heavy boots drinking coffee, just in from fishing on a frigid bay. A large, part-husky dog stands with paws on Art's shoulders, licking his face.

"The *wild* chickens," Art says pontifically, "the *wild* chickens. To the best of my knowledge these are a cross between some kind of fighting bird and some kind of pretty common bird like a bantam. I *do* know this is the eighth generation. Jabe Jackson had a huge tribe of wild chickens. One day he damn near broke his leg trying to capture them, so I said, 'bring some down here, we'll turn 'em loose.'"

The sun in Art's kitchen is bright and hot, belying the freezing temperatures outside and the icy breezes blowing in off Lake Michigan. "You keep animals penned up, 's not right. That's my philosophy. Indians had chickens—partridge was an Indian chicken. But that partridge was free until the moment he died. My philosophy is that it's wrong to hunt and kill anything that isn't necessary for survival. It's not good to pen things up. You take a wild animal from its environment and you tame it, that animal's forever dependent on its domesticator. Its life-style has been altered to such a degree, it can no longer survive in its former mode. The Indian is closely allied to the animals. We're part of the ecosystem. I don't know how a bear feels being in a cage but I've got a pretty good idea."

I ask Art if he feeds the chickens and if he's ever eaten one.

"We don't eat 'em. I guess you could. I get 'em wild birdseed, very little of that. They thrive on it. That's about it. They got their own water. They'll jump up in a tree just like a partridge and eat seeds. I go out and chat with 'em. They go cluck-cluck. They're friendly. Not much to it. Oh, and one other thing, that rooster, every morning, five-thirty on the money, *on the money*." He chuckles.

I leave Art and go down and see the chickens. They're kind of blackie-blue in color with a little brown. They look sentient, beady-eyed, and wiley. It is hard to know for sure if the chickens appreciate Art's philosophy or his sense of humor. Of course they aren't the only beneficiaries. The rest of us—who wince when we buy a chicken and see the little pockets of fat, who sometimes wish to stem the tide of automation and domestication that seems to be sweeping along not only animals but humans in its wake—can find comfort in knowing that the tide is being reversed in some small way from this outpost on the frozen shores of the Grand Traverse Bay.

Personals

The Dunes, My Father

WHEN YOU FIRST see the Sleeping Bear Dunes rising massive and golden two hundred feet above a grassy plain, you think you're in the Serengeti or someplace equally strange, not the Midwest. On its eastern slope, this mountain of flesh-colored sand rises like the Taj Mahal to be mirrored in the placid, cattail-bordered Mill Pond below.

I never thought too much about it, growing up there. When you're a child your environment is your environment; it could be the far side of the moon and you wouldn't think about it. The Sleeping Bear Dunes were where we always took our end-of-the-school-year picnics, the red, white, and blue school buses of the 1950s lining up at the base of the dunes from all over Michigan. It got so that by third grade we'd complain about going to the dunes *again*—as in vanilla ice cream, *again*. We didn't know that our vanilla ice cream was everyone else's pistachio nut ripple.

When the U.S. Army Corps of Engineers first began surveying the land in the dunes in 1957, there were rumblings about a national park some day. This was dismissed as preposterous by most people because everyone knew you didn't put national parks where there were people living. Others thought it was more wishful thinking, grandiose notions, like the one about the mining company that was supposed to come in and mine the sand.

Realists believed no one in his right mind would ever want

that old pile of sand. My father, a lumberman who already owned large tracts of land in and around the dunes, began quietly buying up more duneland, even buying some from the State of Michigan. Most people were only too glad to sell their land in the dunes to anyone fool enough to buy it.

Did my father know about the park coming in? It's not clear. His secretary with whom he was having an affair, an affair that I was privy to and the unwitting beard for at the ages of four and five, was active in the statewide Democratic party. My child's mind was aware only of endless maps, wall-sized blueprints, and the army cot that mysteriously materialized one day in my father's office and that he said he needed for "naps." How much my father's secretary may have lobbied for the park with Democratic senators on the one side, and tipped my father's hand in his land speculation on the other, is not known. What is known is that in all original and final plans her land along the base of the dunes on M-109 was excised from the park. The park boundaries snaked along, encompassing everything in their path, until coming to her land; then, just as if an invisible snag had been hit, the boundaries blipped up and around her land and then back down to the road again a mile later.

In 1961, Democratic Senators Philip Hart and Patrick McNamara, both now deceased, first introduced a national park bill to Congress. At this time public hearings were held around the area. Public sentiment against the park was running high. I can remember my mingled embarrassment and pride as my father—in work boots and wool plaid work shirt—walked onto the stage of the Traverse City High School and demanded, red-faced and using poor grammar, that Senator Hart and "the big boys" in Washington give him and other landowners fair value for their land. How smooth and gracious Senator Hart was by comparison, how schooled in public speaking.

Through all this, local people who hated the idea of, as they phrased it, "the government coming in here and running our lives," saw my father as a champion of capitalism, synonymous in their minds with democracy. My family was staunchly Republican and so was the rest of the community. There is nothing like having the majority on your side to lull you into an unthinking certainty of being right. I mean, does water run uphill?

Back in the classroom at Glen Lake Community School in Maple City, my English teacher assigned us a "paper" on the dunes controversy. He was what people in the community called "an odd duck." He wore his hair longer than most, had students call him "Pete" if they came by his house on weekends, and was the first English teacher I ever had who assigned anything that wasn't in the textbook. He was fired the next year. I liked him and never dreamed he would disapprove when I wrote a paper against the park. He gave me a C +, the lowest grade I ever got from him, and told me to think about it some more.

I've had three decades to think about it since then. And watch it. Just recently I read in the newspaper, in March of 1989, that a group of Glen Arbor citizens got together and purchased non-park land in the village to protect it from development—rampaging development just beyond the boundaries of the park, development that was caused, ironically, by the presence of the national park. This private purchase of land for public use would have been unthinkable thirty years ago; it simply would not have occurred to anyone.

I've seen the issue change, but mainly I've seen the terminology change. My father, who was viewed in the fifties as "a rugged individualist" and "champion of free enterprise," became by the mid-1970s, "a developer." The tide of public opinion changed through the years so the predominant public mood of wanting to fight the bureaucracy became one of wanting to protect the environment. My father went from hero to villain in the public's eyes in the same time period that he made the reverse journey in mine.

In 1974 I came home from New York City and worked for my father managing his scenic drive in the dunes. I was twenty-nine. I had come home from Manhattan emotionally devastated and thirty thousand dollars in debt following a protracted custody battle and divorce. I did not die of cancer, like Debra Winger in *Terms of Endearment,* but I wanted to. My father told me if I could stop crying long enough to rake the four acres in my front yard at the dunes farmhouse, he'd then talk to me about managing the park. I did both, and for the first time in nearly twenty years we were friends again.

He would come into my orange kitchen at 6:00 A.M. and have a cup of coffee and ask how the trucks were running. Was the backhoe holding up? We would talk with the big dunes behind us, outside the long, high farmhouse windows, somnolent in the early morning light. A goddess. Unnamed. But she made her presence felt.

My father was dark, tense, thick-bodied, quiet, sensual. Ours was a silent communication. This was the man who'd taught me awe and joy as a child, simply by pointing. Birds' nests with tiny blue-speckled eggs. Birds' nests with pink, naked, open-mawed hatchlings. Snake babies under rocks. Ants carrying ant eggs in their mouths. Gordian horse hairs swimming in pools. Dappled newborn fawns motionless in dappled sunlight. Trout guts with caddis flies. Gray milt. Pinkish-yellow roe. The single magenta blossom in the center of the million-blossomed head of the Queen Anne's lace. Pitcher thistle. Bearberry. Arbutus. Bloodroot. The red roots of the sweetgrass in the troughs of the interdunal ponds. The way geese coming north in the spring sound like seagulls, high and mewling, and geese going south in the fall sound like a rocking chair, WONKA, WONKA; all business.

One morning he came in and said, "Your mother was a good woman. But she was awful critical of me. At one point she belonged to twelve different clubs and was president of eleven of them." This was a gloss. My father abandoned my mother, leaving her to raise five daughters alone.

In those days I wore shorts and halters until my father told me to "put some clothes on for Chrissake." My father was a female-dependent male. I know because I keep marrying him. He desperately needed and loved women, desperately needed to escape them, too. His mother kept him alive in a shoe box on the back of the wood stove. Women were his "source," and he feared being absorbed by them as much as he was drawn to them.

Everything is connected. My father's personal life and his treatment of my mother were not a separate thing from his land speculation. When I think of the dunes I think of my mother; I think of my father.

My first day on the job my father showed me how to drive the three-quarter-ton truck, the one with the holes in the floor. He took me and my two children, his grandchildren, whom he treated as if they were invisible, up into the shady forests of the back dunes to show us huge red trilliums in bloom.

But we had little contact. "Gran'pa never looks at me," my son said. One morning my daughter said she'd dreamed she'd seen Gran'pa walking up the driveway, bringing a horse on a lead to her. But it never happened.

My children played in the dunes by day, as I had. I knew without asking them how the sand felt like corduroy beneath their feet, how it squeaked. I knew without asking how the dunes were glittery in the daytime heat, heat waves rising like spirits from the sand, diaphanous. At night when the heat went out of the dunes they were cold as ice, dry ice.

One day my father showed up earlier than usual, and he didn't come into the kitchen. I felt, rather than saw, him on my porch. When I pulled on a pair of Levis and a T-shirt and went out onto the still-dark porch, he looked ashen, his skin the color of creek marl. It was August. I looked past him to the yard, at the trees and grass, then back. August is an odd time; the light is odd, making everything look like an overexposed color photo, the grass too yellow, the green trees black-green.

"Cindy died," he said.

So taciturn was my father, so closemouthed, that he almost expected to communicate by ESP, and almost did. It took me several minutes to recall that he had a black lab named Cindy.

"She was floating in the trout pond this morning," he said. His whole personality, or person, had a leaden quality, like weather waiting for rain. He said his wife had left the day before to go shopping downstate. He said it appeared Cindy had died of a heart attack.

My father had a second wife. He had not married his secretary after all, a small, dark Southern woman who'd stayed married to her husband. He had miraculously found another big-boned, tall, redheaded woman, almost identical to my mother in physical type, but unlike her in having an affinity for guns, hunting, and training dogs. She had been married to a doctor, an anesthesiologist, who'd committed suicide by shooting himself in the head on a deserted road. She had a martial quality.

My father's big black Buick sat shiny on the gravel driveway. I looked from the car shining in the sun to him in the shadow of my porch. He looked odd to me, oddly weakened. At moments like this I forgave him everything. Forgave him leaving my mother, forgave him for walking away from me and my four sisters. Saw us all as intimate strangers sucked into the brutality of materialism, how we sold ourselves into marriage, into myriad forms of oppression for the sake of procreating, of surviving. My redhaired mother, a burning bush. My father, rain. The dog's death. The shadow of the thing, rather than the thing. It is not this; it is not that. It isn't the first thing; it isn't the second thing. It is all everything.

It was Cindy's death and the way my father had looked that had me in the blackberries, picking berries for a pie for his birthday September third. But he died. Suddenly and bizarrely, the day before his sixty-ninth birthday and the day after the United States government had awarded him three-and-a-half million dollars for his land in the dunes. Heart attack. His wife was in town shopping. A young boy with him had called the ambulance, but by the time it came the thirty miles from Kalkaska, he was dead.

"John Law," my father's wife kept saying and putting her arm around the shoulders of my then companion, a Leelanau County sheriff's deputy, "John Law. We have John Law here to take care of us." She rambled, going on about how her first husband had always cleaned his guns so carefully.

My father was buried in the hot, dry Kalkaska ground. Evergreen Cemetery. The undertaker had a pallor like that of his client, as if he had put powder over his five o'clock shadow. The service was Catholic, although my father was not. My mother attended at a distance, dry-eyed and resolute. My sisters flew in from all over the country and left again. It was not our style to sit around and talk and drink, and so we didn't.

I did not see my father again until November when his apparition accompanied me on the way to cut the Christmas tree up in the dunes. He didn't talk, which was normal, but simply walked along beside me, going up and over the furrows of the rows of planted Christmas trees.

I never saw his widow again. She moved to Sun City, Arizona. I never visited his home again. His house burned down six months after he died; burned to the ground before the fire trucks could arrive. I never saw the woman he had an affair with, his secretary, again either. But one day when I was living in Traverse City I called an ad in the classified section of the *Preview*, a shopping weekly. There was an ad for a waffle iron. When I called the woman, she said it was like new and only ten dollars. She asked my name and when I told her she said she was my father's old secretary, that she was disabled and couldn't drive. She said I should come and get the waffle iron, that if she could drive she'd bring it to me. She said she'd give it to me for nothing. That it would be free. If I'd come and get it. She was insistent, sticky, like insect legs caught in wool.

For days the image of this old crone kept coming back to me, this ghost from the past, fluttering her old lady's handkerchief at me across the years, a tiny speck on the horizon behind me, her tiny voice saying, "come and get the waffle iron." I pictured her in her wheelchair, all the raw passion for land and sex gone. My father, too, gone, his life measured more by what his mistresses did him out of than by his daughters, his grandchildren, his wonderful, visionary sense of land. His body, like an outdated piece of machinery, rusting in the ground, the primal urges and the transcendent alike, equally dead.

Only the dunes stay, glittery in the noonday heat and cold

under the stars at night. Mythic, monumental, mysterious, the dunes lie like a lovely lady napping, waiting to inspire the next insignificant mortal to take a run at her heights, her steep slopes, her massiveness, her soft yet hard gemlike beauty, her ability to not only outlast, but confound, those who would try to possess her.

What Napoleon Needed

I LIVE WHERE I LIVE because it puts me in touch with everyday life. Everyday life in a country setting where people still talk to each other is the compass I take my bearings from. With all its imprecisions, ambiguities, contradictions, and outrages, it is still all we have, or it is *what we have*.

Today is a typical day in my life. I get up at 3:00 A.M. to put wood in the stove. I wait for the logs to catch and stand watching the snow fall on the pond. I go back to bed and do not wake up until 5:00 A.M. There is a faint sound of music. At first I think it's the clock radio, then realize it's our three-year-old upstairs in her bed singing "Jingle Bells" very softly.

My husband and I are in a good mood this morning because he is home an hour longer. He has a dental appointment in Traverse City at 8:30 A.M. and will go to work after that, which means he can leave home at 7:30 A.M. instead of 6:30 A.M. I ask his opinion about what our youngest should wear for her school picture today. He says, "Something she wants to wear. That way there will be less trouble dressing her." I tell him he is a pragmatist, but he corrects me and says he is a realist. "Pragmatism suggests I've made deals with life. Maybe I have, but I resent the implication." This is our way of joking around.

At 9:00 A.M. I am trotting down the walk to the Leland Community Nursery School and Daycare Center. The sidewalks are snow-covered and slippery. I walk carefully. I think I probably look like a duck. I see several people here I have seen at other places around town: the mechanic from Van's garage, Geoff's father; the vegetable girl from the grocery store, Michael and Joey's mother; a teacher from the public school, Billy's mother. I like being in this human web of people at this hour in the morning. I like being in this little toy town with its church steeples and hills and wind off Lake Michigan and townspeople who know each other.

In the parking lot of the nursery school I talk to my friend Mary. She is pregnant. She had gone into convulsions earlier in the week and now is afraid of miscarrying. She looks pale and thin and I am concerned for her. But we talk of other things: kids, holiday plans, boot styles.

By 9:30 A.M. I am in the Lake Leelanau Post Office picking up my mail. I may see several people I usually see only here at the post office: Linda Harrison, wife of the writer, Jim Harrison; Ted Grant, owner of the post office building; Byron Belknap, husband of a woman in prison; George Shaw, a poet-woodcutter. Sometimes I see Ed Plamondon, a farmer whose daughter was friends with my sister; Ed boarded my sister's horse for her. We are all in the same or overlapping traffic patterns. We nod our hellos and head for home, or for the grocery store across the street, N.J.'s, where we nod hello again.

Ostensibly I am a writer and I work at home, but since I do work at home, other things weave into this. While I am trying to think of how to begin something, I empty the ashes in the wood stove and fold laundry. If I still can't think of anything, I go for a walk. Usually finding distractions is not a problem, because when you work at home people drop by all the time on the assumption that writing isn't really work, and since you're writing, you aren't busy doing anything else. I think this is about right.

Mid-morning sometime my mother comes by. She is wearing a red and gray plaid mohair coat with three-quarter-length dolman sleeves and an attached scarf, a gray fedora with a red feather, gray gloves, and gray half-boots in the latest fashion. She is on her way to visit a friend who is dying. For a minute I

think she is overdressed and then I think, overdressed for what? Her fashionable attire is her innately elegant and dignified stance in the face of the grittiness of life and the relentlessness of death. Her friend has been hallucinating for three days. This is the fifth one of my mother's friends to die in a year.

My friend Archie is on the phone. He wants to know how I make my egg bread, or Challah. I tell him the ingredients. While Archie and I are on the phone, my friend Laurie comes by to pick up some tablecloths. She is hosting twenty-five people for a holiday dinner. "I thought we were only going to have about ten people, but I keep inviting people. I don't want anyone to feel left out."

At 12:30 P.M. I pick up my three-year-old from nursery school. It is 1:30 P.M. before she finally falls asleep upstairs after snacks, stories, a glass of water, and three minutes of talking about what she calls "important things."

At 3:30 P.M. my fourteen-year-old gets off the school bus. She is very upset. A boy in her school has committed suicide.

He shot himself. This is the third teenage suicide in the county in six months. "He was pretty normal," my daughter says. "Kids liked him. His parents weren't divorced or anything."

At 4:30 P.M. Ruthie Grote drops off her son Johnnie's goldfish. The Grotes are going to St. Louis, and my older daughter has agreed to take care of the goldfish. It is a tiny goldfish in a tiny bowl. She says, "I can't believe I'm babysitting for a goldfish."

At 5:30 P.M. my husband comes home from work. He takes our three-year-old sledding on the hill in front of our house for an hour. Then we have a light supper. It is Friday, and we are meeting friends at the Bay Theater in Suttons Bay to see *Napoleon*. Our friends are Napoleon buffs and say this is supposed to be a fantastic movie: it was sold out in Detroit when they were down there.

It is snowing heavily. All the street lights have halos. We go in and see a three-hour Napoleon movie. When we come out, it is still snowing heavily. Napoleon, I think to myself as we walk, could have used a few hundred doses of everyday life.

High School Reunion

THIS IS A STORY about a high school reunion, that time called the sixties, and a northern Michigan peninsula. Let's begin with the place, the Leelanau Peninsula, because that is what I always think of first—that place where high hills sheer off the land at the water's edge on the Lake Michigan side of the peninsula, and cherry orchards slope gently down toward the bay on the other.

We've been compared to the boot of Italy, the way it reaches out into the Mediterranean, how you're always aware of being surrounded by a large body of water. We've been compared, too, to California's Monterey Peninsula, a Michigan Eden with our trilliums and northern lights—only six hours away from Detroit. We are like those places and we aren't. We are northern: colder, more delicate, more geologically new; sand dunes and gravelly hills. And the glaciers that rolled over us as recently as ten thousand years ago, and several times before that, left us a dozen deep inland lakes, scattered in between the hills like afterthoughts.

My class was the class of '63. Why do I have such a sense of lost innocence when I say that? Maybe it's because my peninsula, always a rural backwater when I was growing up, has been discovered by the developers. Maybe it's because we of the sixties came of age in the fifties, thinking we would grow into the world of our older brothers and sisters: sock hops, Elvis, '57 Chevies, drive-in movies, cherry Cokes, prom night, and lilacs in the gym when we graduated.

I remember a rainy November Saturday in the fifties, deer season, going with my two older sisters over to a place in Honor called the Green Lantern and drinking forbidden coffee and listening to Pat Boone sing, "Love Letters in the Sand," and imagining in the way only a twelve-year-old can that some day I would step into their world of secrets and sophistication.

Somewhere between then and the time I graduated I lost that desire. I discovered Lawrence Ferlinghetti, James Joyce, and Jack Kerouac. I began to believe I was more sophisticated than my sisters. I began to listen to jazz. I stayed home from school and read *Finnegan's Wake* and drank Harvey's Bristol Cream Sherry and felt myself to be bored and decadent and, as I would have said at the time, "filled with ennui."

I stayed home and read James Joyce so often during my junior year that I managed to fail nearly everything. I thought this was a measure of my ennui. So did my parents, and my senior year I went to live with my sister in Buffalo, New York, and attended Amherst High School. My sister taught at the Jesuit-run Canisius College; I fancied myself a college student, too, and attended dress rehearsals for Brendan Behan plays and heard Norman Mailer speak, and Allen Ginsberg. A bureaucratic sleight of hand allowed me to technically graduate from Glen Lake High School on the Leelanau Peninsula. This way I could be an in-state student at the University of Michigan. My last memory of high school on the Leelanau Peninsula is being poured into a dreadful electric blue satin sheath dress that had belonged to my sister Pat and attending graduation ceremonies in the Glen Lake gym. No lilacs, or at least I don't remember them.

You can imagine how I felt when I got the announcement about the high school reunion. Always having cringed at the memory of myself as an awkward, prepubescent twelve-year-old or self-dramatizing sixteen-year-old, I was reluctant to traipse back to the high school reunion. I couldn't quite put my finger on what it was that made me uncomfortable. Maybe it was that high school reunions seemed like such a fifties thing to do, prom king and prom queen. More likely it was that I thought I didn't "fit in" with whatever it was I imagined my classmates to be.

I think I was wrong on both counts. Reunions are timeless. They don't belong to the eras they commemorate, but are real benchmarks, a way for everyone to check in, to see where everyone else is, has been, is going, so they can know where they are themselves. Secondly, and how I could have missed this I don't know, while I was rebelling, my classmates were rebelling too. They had often broken with convention, or were tolerant of people who did. It was the hallmark of our generation.

I'd run into several of my classmates through the years, and they were remarkably open and nonjudgmental. Perhaps this is because the generation that came of age in the sixties saw such incredible cultural change. We had Vietnam veterans in our class as well as protesters of the Vietnam War. We had seen saving-ourselves-for-marriage give way to Free Love, give way to AIDS. As a group, we'd been through a lot. The set of values we'd grown up with—who'd been raised on farms and who'd grown up in town; who was married and who was divorced; who had babies before they were married and who had church weddings and babies later; who had money and who didn't— just simply didn't matter to the people in my class. We'd been through too much; all bets were off. We cared for each other. That was all; that was enough.

The day of the high school reunion dawned pink and cold, a cross between winter and summer, frost on the grass in the morning and shirtsleeve weather by afternoon. Sugarloaf Mountain Resort, where the dinner dance with sixties deejay was to be, is about ten miles from my house. I spent the day hanging wash on the line, which I never do, almost as if I was preparing to step back in time.

I feel like a movie star when I arrive at Sugarloaf. Don't ask me why. Not because I look like one. I think it's because I've worn a 1940s-style dress and because I feel like I'm pretending to be both myself and another, younger self.

Jill Baxter is here and when I see her I realize she looks like Mae West, and always did. She is married, remarried; two kids. I learn for the first time that she'd had an unhappy home life growing up, and I'd always thought her life was perfect. She says she'd thought the same thing about me, mostly because our family had a library. I thought her family was perfect because they had cows. Now this shows you what children know.

Jill and I both decide that if we had it to do over again, we'd be flat-chested. How did we get so many big-bosomed girls in one class? Almost as if we'd programmed our puberty before we'd had time to see how the zeitgeist would change. We'd gone from Mae West to Mia Farrow since we'd come of age. Suzy Schmidt was philosophical about it. She said she figured that by the time she was an old lady everything would have settled around her ankles, which was okay, because it would help hold her to the ground.

George Clausen Dechow is here, Jill's cousin. We'd always called him G. K. He was, as we said back then, "an only child." In our little community of good breeders, this was practically unheard of, and we determined, in our cruel and childish way, that it made G. K. "different." Now there are lots of only children, and G. K., who was and is the soul of kindness, has turned into a prince. He's thin and handsome, a wonderful dancer, has a wife and two kids in Kansas City. He has a big house, six times the size of mine; it probably has a library.

G. K. says he feels "good, strange" about being there, which is how a lot of people say they feel about being there and seeing their old classmates. With someone else, either Janice Olson or Jill Baxter, we decide that the whole experience of a high school reunion is like running into an old friend in an airport, having lunch, and then getting on separate planes for separate lives, forever.

"You know, I hated it here," says Judy Dechow, Jill's sister. She is far and away one of the most beautiful women there, a tiny waist with a rhinestone belt, black dress, braces; she looks eighteen. "I had all bad memories. Then I come back here. I see people who care about each other. They reach out to one another. They work hard. They're real. This is where reality is. Not the plastic world I just came from. These people know how to be friends. They accept you. They aren't judgmental."

She sums up a lot of what I feel. I remember, as if it had only been yesterday, Jerry Barzcak and Carl Olson making fun of how I could never hit the ball with the bat, and then gallantly taking my last strike so I could run the bases. The deal was this: whichever team had to take me, the best hitter on the other team would take my third strike, honor-bound to hit well, so that I could at least run the bases like the others.

We are all eager to be kind to each other that night at the high school reunion. "In order," as my friend Suzy Schmidt said later over lunch in Traverse City, "to make up for being snotty as kids." And one can't always even remember whom one was snotty to, or why, and so it's best to be nice as pie to everyone.

Time, like the glaciers that rolled over our peninsula, has obliterated certain landmark memories but created others. We look around at each other; we are the same, yet different. We are slightly altered on the surface, as the peninsula itself had been altered by development, but the feeling of recognition is still there, profoundly there.

In the end, like characters in Proust's *Remembrance of Things Past,* will we have mainly memories of each other, more tangible perhaps than the reality?

Carl Olson looks the same, yet different. The baseball player. He sells insurance in Lansing. He is well off. His wife is beautiful. He has kind eyes. He says he bought the old Peppler place on Glen Lake. "It's funny," he tells me, "how this peninsula gets in your blood. Eighteen years in one place. I know where to hunt or fish or hike."

Martin Basch, class president. He went to the University of Michigan at the same time I did. He's a lawyer now. I envy him his solidity. He envies me the chances I took. When we were in Ann Arbor I knew radicals who wanted to know people who worked in factories, people they called "workers." Martin was a worker in a factory, a worker in fact working himself through law school. He saw his life as a deep trough, a life that never allowed him to look over the sides. I see his life as honorable.

I spent nearly every day of my life with almost all of these people for nearly eighteen years, and it strikes me that night, as I dance with some and talk with others, that as the evening passes, it's almost as if no time has elapsed. My Ferlinghetti stage was only a stage after all, not the final word on who I am or was. I could see these people again in heaven and still find I am closer to them, know them better, than all the people in between, or I could see them again in my next life and recognize them. In heaven or in my next life, whichever comes first, we will meet again, I feel as the evening ends.

Dreaming Detroit

DETROIT LOOMS in the dead of winter up north like an oasis of civilization somewhere to the south of us. Whatever Detroit's image is to the rest of the country, or even to Detroiters, to a northern Michiganian with cabin fever, Detroit is a fantastic city filled with possibilities.

There's a certain time of year up here when there is nothing to do and nowhere to go, nothing but bars and basketball games and more of the same. If you aren't ready yet to drink your brains out, you stay home. Snow extends for miles in every direction, and one lives literally in a vacuum. A new curtain of snow descends hourly around one's small house, and the sense that there is, three hundred miles to the south, a city, is the one counterbalance to gaping infinity.

I cannot complain, as Ovid did when Caesar exiled him to some awful jumping-off place on the shores of the Black Sea, that I am trapped in among the barbarians, "those gross tribes that sweep down from the steppes." I am, in some sense, one of those barbarians, having grown up here in the crossroads settlement of Glen Arbor on the shores of Lake Michigan. In the vernacular of the summer people, I am a "local." And while I may have been trapped here as a child, nothing forced me to come back here as an adult.

My roots drew me back here, but no sooner was I here than I longed for everything I had gone away to find: jobs, money, education, art, people like me, people not like me, drama, diversity, energy—in short, civilization.

Civilization, I've come to understand over the years, is having enough people interacting in one spot over a period of time to give life definition and make it interesting. Living in the vast north country, you face one awesome truth: when a tree falls in the forest and nobody hears it, nobody cares.

As a child living on a high hill above Lake Michigan, I would watch the freighters go by on their way to those far-off magazine and movie cities known collectively as civilization. Just as Detroiters fantasize about the piney Michigan that stretches due north of them and come to view it—romantically and somewhat erroneously—as a world of wood stoves, log cabins, and trout streams, I have spent a lifetime dreaming Detroit. Mainly my impressions of Detroit, like a kindergartner's ideas about where babies come from, have been garnered secondhand from books and ex-Detroiters, a fanciful amalgam that most real Detroiters probably would find amusing but unrecognizable.

So let's imagine we have just met, at the trout stream in front of my log cabin, and are becoming fast friends. Let's throw another log on the fire, put a pot of coffee on the wood stove, and I'll bring out the vignettes and freeze-frame images of Detroit I've collected over the years the way a tourist collects Petoskey stones.

Aunt Myrtle provided me with my earliest impressions of Detroit. She was a redheaded woman who had chartreuse Chinese coolies on her what-not shelf and who painted her nails. Aunt Myrtle knew how to play canasta and once played it with me for a week. "She's from Detroit," my mother said often about Aunt Myrtle. I didn't know what this meant, exactly—that Aunt Myrtle dared to be different because she was from Detroit, or that everyone in Detroit painted their nails and played canasta—but I wanted to find out.

Another time my mom and my Aunt Carol packed about six of us kids into the station wagon and went on a marathon shopping trip, less to Detroit than to downtown Hudson's. After a whirlwind tour of a dozen floors of goods, by escalator and elevator and with all of us in tow, we ended up waist-deep in a city pool in hot July, my aunt and my mother remarking

on how much they'd had to pay for all of us to go swimming. What possessed these two women to drive almost three hundred miles to look at towels and why they didn't leave us home, I will never know. I suppose they had no choice but to take us, and it was simply "the call" of Hudson's echoing back past Clare, rippling up and over the cedar swamps, that finally caused them to get in the car and *go*.

Detroit is a place where people either made history or were aware of it being made and therefore participated vicariously in events beyond themselves even when they didn't participate directly. I still can see Hervey Parke, a relative of the people who owned the old Parke Pharmaceutical Company in Detroit, sitting on the porch of his Lake Michigan home, telling me how his great-uncle, Captain Hervey Parke, had walked out from New York State to survey along the Detroit River. "He walked with a forty-five-pound pack on his back," Hervey said. "People walked then, you know."

I cultivate Detroiters, which isn't hard to do in an area to which they all seem to be moving. One day my stove broke and the Sears man came to fix it. He was and is a real Detroiter whose grandfather was a motorman on the Detroit Street Railway in the days when you could go anywhere in the city on the DSR for a nickel. "I grew up on Detroit's East Side," Ken Dezur says. "Linnhurst. Fairmont, when the streets were gravel. From Fairmont to Eight Mile it was all open fields. We could sit on the upstairs porch and watch the fireworks at Eastwood Park on the Fourth of July. On warm summer nights my folks used to take us kids out to Belle Isle to sleep in the grass. Tashmo Park. New Baltimore. It was like the wilderness. We used to swim off the dock in the St. Clair River. The current was real strong there." He draws an impromptu map while he waits for the timer to go off on my stove. "You have Lake Erie, then the Detroit River, Lake St. Clair, the St. Clair River, and Lake Huron." The drawing is gone, but the place that stays in my mind is this city, where a kid could go anywhere for a nickel, a city surrounded by a river with a strong current. The excitement of participation, that's what Detroit had to offer, and maybe that's why my aunt and my mother drove three hundred miles—to be caught up in the current of others' lives.

Marianne Russell is a friend of mine who grew up in Detroit. "I remember riding in the elevator at Hudson's," she tells me one gray November day in Glen Arbor, when we are trying to think of ways to keep her magazine afloat in an area where there are no people to buy ads. "I remember being four feet tall, and all I could see were rear ends and the bottom buttons of people's coats. I remember art classes at the Detroit Institute of Arts, Saturday morning, huddled in the cold outside those wrought-iron gates. I remember the man in the Kern block on Woodward, standing on a crate, quoting from the Bible, dressed in a big black topcoat and a white silk scarf." Detroit was a place with enough people, she seemed to be saying, to allow characters and creativity to flourish, to allow art and culture to flourish, to be crowded in an elevator—enough people to buy ads.

At a party one night recently during an early spring thaw, when the water was dripping rhythmically off the eaves and the melting snow seemed to make the air heady with oxygen, Sue Kopka tells me about growing up in Bloomfield Hills. "When my parents moved there in the 1960s," she says, "Bloomfield Hills was the country. It was woods and farm fields and swamp. Now I go back there and it's gone. It's city now. There was a huge twisted tree, like a serpent, that we played on as kids, next to the swamp. Now the tree is gone. The swamp is gone. I came north to find country, to come home. But sometimes I wonder what would have happened if we had all stayed living where we grew up. We would have felt more attached to the land, and we might have fought to save it."

In some ways we are all a nation of nomads—restless, displaced, haunted by memories of trees and men with Bibles, yuppies looking for the perfect place—not realizing we create our environment as much as it creates us. The difference is that here in the north country all the ingredients are raw, like a new bolt of cloth, whereas in Detroit it's a matter of remaking what's already been done. In the north we have to figure out ways to create civilization without destroying the wilderness. In Detroit the dilemma is to recreate some wilderness without perturbing two million people.

The proper balance of civilization and country living seems to be what everyone is looking for. And almost in the space of time that we've been talking by our imaginary trout stream, or certainly since I was growing up here forty years ago, civilization, with all its paved roads, water pollution, traffic, condominiums, and hundreds of people, has moved north. As I watch

the wilderness vanish, it strikes me as odd that in all my dreaming of Detroit, I had always imagined I would go there; I never
dreamed it would come to me.